So Easy, So Delicious

Be sure to visit
www.EllieDeaner.com
for more recipes.

12/25/02

To Pam,
Happy cooking!
Ellie Deaner

To my husband, Dennis,
and my sons, Jonathan, Robert and Joshua

Strategic consulting: Jonathan Deaner
Design: Ann Gillespie
Cover photograph: Sue Anne Hodges

Also by Ellie Deaner:
From Ellie's Kitchen To Yours

So Easy,
So Delicious

ELLIE DEANER

Denell Press
P.O. Box 1164
Framingham, Massachusetts 01701

So Easy, So Delicious

By Ellie Deaner

Published by:

Denell Press
Post Office Box 1164
Framingham, MA 01701-1164 U.S.A.

Publisher's Cataloging-in-Publication
(Provided by Quality Books, Inc.)

Deaner, Ellie.
    So easy, so delicious : Ellie's latest foolproof
cooking hints and recipes from appetizers and salads to main
courses and desserts. -- 1st ed.
      p. cm.
    Includes index.
    Preassigned LCCN: 98-96593
    ISBN: 0-9631177-3-4

    1. Cookery. 2. Quick and easy cookery. I. Title.

TX714.D43 1999   641.5
                                   QB198-1380

10 9 8 7 6 5 4 3 2 1
First Edition

Contents

Introduction

I was inspired to write this cookbook as a result of the overwhelming enthusiasm that I felt in response to my first one, From Ellie's Kitchen To Yours. Wherever I am, people constantly approach me with stories. They say that their dinner parties were successes because of my recipes. Or they mention that even though they've been cooking for years, they can always open up my book and be sure to find a recipe that adds zip to their repertoire. One of my favorite things to hear is that someone who had always been afraid to cook now loves to do so because my cookbook gave them confidence. But the most popular comment is that all of the recipes are "so easy and so delicious." (What a great title for my next cookbook, I thought!)

My passions for cooking, sharing recipes and teaching others are the reasons why I decided to write my cookbooks. I feel that everyone is entitled to enjoy good food regardless of dietary restrictions and that almost everyone is capable of cooking when given a cookbook with a straightforward approach. That's why I always strive to write the recipes with easy-to-follow directions along with adaptation suggestions for all kinds of diets and lifestyles.

The kitchen is the heart of my home. It's where I spend the majority of my day doing what I love best—cooking. My kitchen is where my family and friends gather to enjoy conversation, laughter and good food. It is my hope that this book will inspire you to engage in the pleasure of cooking and share your results with your loved ones.

There are so many people I'd like to thank for their interest and assistance while I wrote this book: my husband, an unending source of encouragement who helped me in so many ways that I could not list them; my cooking students and friends, who expressed a desire for more recipes, so willingly shared favorites and made the sacrifice to be taste testers; my parents and sister, who offered endless support; and my sons who enthusiastically provided suggestions and guidance—I am thrilled that each of them derives pleasure from cooking.

I hope you enjoy using this book. May all of your meals be easy and delicious!

Ingredients and Substitutions

Black pepper: Freshly ground is preferable to that in a spice jar.

Broth: Canned or granulated beef, chicken, fish and vegetable broth may be substituted for homemade.

Cheese: You can substitute low fat varieties for many kinds of cheese.

Cream: All-purpose, medium, heavy or whipping cream can be used interchangeably.

Eggs: Always use large unless specified otherwise.

Flour: Always use all-purpose, unless specified otherwise.

Garlic: Whenever possible, use fresh.

Herbs: Whenever possible, use fresh.

Lemon juice: Whenever possible, use fresh.

Lemon, orange or lime rind or zest: Whenever possible, use fresh. Use a lemon zester to remove rind from fruit.

Mayonnaise: You can substitute low fat or low cholesterol versions for regular mayonnaise.

Milk: You can often substitute nonfat or low fat for whole milk.

Nonstick cooking spray: Use to reduce fat and save time.

Nutmeg: For best flavor, grate fresh nutmeg with a nutmeg grater.

Parmesan cheese: Whenever possible, use freshly ground.

Salt, to taste: Season with salt according to your own taste and dietary guidelines.

Sour cream: You can often substitute reduced fat or fat free sour cream or nonfat yogurt.

Sugar: Means granulated white, unless specified otherwise.

Yogurt: You can use nonfat instead of low fat. You can usually substitute yogurt for buttermilk, sour milk or sour cream.

Special Notes:

- In all recipes using an oven, it is assumed that the oven has been preheated, unless specified otherwise.
- Portion sizes are generally not given because they are dependent upon the other dishes served during the meal. Also, appetites and dietary needs vary greatly.

Recipes featured on cover (left to right, front to back):

Pizza (pg. 134)
Chicken With Lemon and Soy Sauce (pg. 105)
Sour Cream Coffee Cake (pg. 160)
Tomato Soup (pg. 28)
Stir-Fry Chicken With Vegetables (pg. 105)
Crustless Vegetable Quiche (pg. 68)
Spinach Salad With Strawberries (pg. 44)
Black Bean and Corn Salad (pg. 45)
Biscotti (pg. 172)
Butterflies or Bows (pg. 171)
Chocolate Slice-and-Bake Cookies (pg. 168)

APPETIZERS

Cheese Crispies

$\frac{1}{2}$ lb butter or margarine, softened
8 oz sharp Cheddar cheese, grated
$1\frac{1}{3}$ C flour

$\frac{1}{8}$ tsp cayenne pepper
2 C crispy rice cereal
Salt, to taste

Cream butter or margarine and mix with grated cheese. Add flour and cayenne pepper. Mix well. Fold in cereal and salt. Drop by teaspoonfuls onto greased baking sheets. Bake at 350° for approximately 15 minutes, or until golden.

Yield: 5 dozen crispies

Hint: *These are delicious served warm or at room temperature. They may be made in advance and frozen or stored in a tin for up to 1 week.*

Shortcut Pesto Rounds

$\frac{1}{2}$ C basil leaves, packed, finely chopped
1 clove garlic, finely minced
$\frac{1}{2}$ C Parmesan cheese, grated

2 T mayonnaise
1 loaf French bread (or baguette) cut into
(18) $\frac{1}{4}$" slices

Combine all ingredients, except bread, in a food processor or blender until smooth. Transfer to a covered container and refrigerate until serving time. This will keep in the refrigerator for a few days. Place bread slices on a cookie sheet or broiler pan and broil for about 1 minute. Turn over and spread untoasted side with basil mixture. Broil for 2 to 3 additional minutes, or until golden.

Yield: 18 rounds

Hint: *Instead of using French bread, you can buy 1- to $1\frac{1}{2}$-inch square toasts, spread the pesto on them and broil.*

■ ■

Reuben Roll-Ups

8 oz lean corned beef
1 C refrigerated sauerkraut (not
  canned), well drained
1 C Swiss cheese, shredded
1 tsp horseradish, or to taste

$\frac{1}{3}$ C Russian or Thousand Island
  salad dressing
$\frac{1}{2}$ tsp caraway seeds (optional)
(2) 8 oz pkgs refrigerated crescent rolls
1 egg, beaten with 1 tsp water

Chop corned beef and sauerkraut in a food processor or with a knife. Add cheese, salad dressing, horseradish and caraway seeds. Open crescent roll packages. Press 2 triangles of dough together and roll out slightly with rolling pin into an oblong shape. Spread one-eighth of this mixture onto each piece of dough. Roll up, jellyroll fashion, and pinch ends to seal. Place seam-side down onto a greased cookie sheet. Brush with egg mixture. Bake at 375° for 12 to 15 minutes, or until golden. Allow to cool for 2 to 3 minutes before slicing. Slice each roll into 8 pieces.

Yield: 64 roll-ups

Hint: You can serve extra Russian or Thousand Island dressing on the side as a dip for the roll-ups. This recipe is very versatile because it can be used as an appetizer, as a light supper or for brunch.

Mushroom Crescents

1 T butter or margarine
1$\frac{1}{2}$ C (6 oz) mushrooms, chopped
1 small onion, chopped
1 tsp flour

$\frac{1}{4}$ tsp thyme
Dash cayenne pepper
8 oz pkg refrigerated crescent rolls
1 egg, beaten with 1 tsp water

Melt butter or margarine in a fry pan. Add mushrooms and onions and sauté until soft. Add flour, thyme and cayenne and stir. Remove from heat and cool. Open crescent roll package and separate triangles. Cut each triangle in half lengthwise. Using a rolling pin, roll out to enlarge each half. Place a dab of filling mixture on wide end of triangle. Roll up towards point and place seam-side down on a greased cookie sheet. Brush with egg mixture. Bake at 400° for 10 to 12 minutes, or until golden.

Yield: 16 crescents

Hint: You can freeze these after they are baked and cooled. To reheat, place in a preheated 350° oven and bake for 10 minutes, or until hot.

Corned Beef or Pastrami Tidbits

$\frac{1}{2}$ to $\frac{3}{4}$ lb corned beef brisket
  or pastrami, sliced

8 oz can whole water chestnuts
$\frac{1}{2}$ C brown sugar, or as needed

Rinse and drain water chestnuts. Cut them in half. Place a water chestnut half on the end of a slice of corned beef or pastrami. Roll up so that the entire water chestnut is enclosed. Fasten with a toothpick and dip both sides of tidbit in brown sugar. Place on a greased broiler pan and broil until slightly browned.

Hint: *These can be assembled a few hours in advance and refrigerated. Broil just before serving.*

Hot Salmon Dip

$14\frac{1}{2}$ oz can red salmon, drained
  and deboned
8 oz whipped cream cheese

1 T Worcestershire sauce
$\frac{1}{4}$ C Cheddar cheese, shredded

With an electric mixer or food processor, blend salmon, cream cheese and Worcestershire sauce very well. Place in a pie plate or ovenproof casserole and sprinkle Cheddar cheese on top. Bake at 350° for 20 minutes, or until golden and puffy. Serve hot with crackers or mini-rye bread.

Cheesy Caper Bites

1 C mayonnaise
8 oz sharp or extra sharp Cheddar
  cheese, shredded

$3\frac{1}{2}$ oz jar capers, drained
6 English muffins, split

Combine mayonnaise and cheese. Gently fold in capers. Spread mixture on English muffin halves. Cut halves into quarters. Place on a cookie sheet. Broil or bake at 400° to 425° for about 10 minutes, or until golden. These can also be frozen. To serve, remove from freezer and bake as above.

Yield: 48 pieces

Hint: *This mixture, which can be made a few days ahead, can be spread on muffins several hours in advance of serving. Bake when needed.*

■ ■

Empanadas

Dough:

6 oz cream cheese
$\frac{1}{2}$ lb butter or margarine

2 C flour

Filling:

I lb ground beef
I egg, beaten
Sweet relish, to taste

Chili sauce, to taste
Garlic powder, to taste
Onion powder, to taste

Eggwash:

I egg, combined with I T water

To Make Dough:

Soften cream cheese and butter or margarine and cream together. Add flour and beat until well mixed. Roll into a ball and wrap in plastic wrap. Refrigerate for several hours or overnight.

To Make Filling and Assemble:

Brown beef and drain fat. Add egg and remaining ingredients, to taste. Cool. Remove dough from refrigerator and divide in half. Keep half in the refrigerator and roll out the other half into a rectangle. Using a $2\frac{1}{2}$- to 3-inch round cookie cutter, make circles of dough. Place I teaspoon of filling on one side of each circle and fold other side of dough over it to form a turnover. Press all around the edges of turnover with tines of a fork. Brush with eggwash. Remove second half of dough from refrigerator and repeat. Bake at 400° on a greased cookie sheet for 15 minutes, or until golden.

Hint: *These may be cooked, cooled and then frozen. Just before serving, pop into a 350° oven for approximately 15 minutes, or until hot. Serve with chili sauce or salsa. Instead of this dough, feel free to substitute another double pie crust.*

■ ■

Onion Cheese Squares

6 T butter or margarine, divided
12 oz onions (3 medium), diced
3 C all-purpose baking
  mix (i.e. Bisquick)
2 C milk

2 eggs
10 oz extra sharp shredded Cheddar
  cheese, divided
2 T poppy seeds

Melt all the butter or margarine in a fry pan. Remove 4 tablespoons and reserve in a small dish. Add the onions to the fry pan and sauté until they are soft and translucent. Combine the baking mix, milk, eggs and all but 4 tablespoons of the cheese in a large bowl. Fold in the cooked onions. Spread this mixture into a well-greased $10\frac{1}{2}''$x$15\frac{1}{2}''$x$1''$ pan and brush with the reserved melted butter or margarine. Sprinkle with reserved cheese and poppy seeds. Bake at 400° for 22 to 26 minutes, or until golden. Cool for a few minutes and then cut into squares.

Yield: 56 squares

Hint: *These freeze very well. Flash freeze the squares on a pan in the freezer. When they are frozen, pull them off the pan and place them in a plastic bag. Then you can take out just the amount that you need when you want a quick hors d'oeuvre. Heat at 350° for about 10 minutes, or until hot.*

Greek Meatballs

2 lbs ground beef or lamb
1 C bread crumbs
1 large onion, finely minced
$\frac{1}{2}$ C water
1 egg
$\frac{3}{4}$ tsp cinnamon

$\frac{1}{2}$ to 1 tsp salt, or to taste
Black pepper, to taste
2 tsp oregano
1 tsp garlic powder
1 tsp parsley, finely chopped
Few T flour, for rolling meatballs

In a large bowl, blend all ingredients together except flour. Mix lightly and roll into 1-inch balls. Roll lightly in flour. Place balls on 2 greased cookie sheets and bake at 350° for 40 to 45 minutes, turning occasionally so that they brown evenly. Serve hot or cold as an appetizer.

Yield: approx. $5\frac{1}{2}$ dozen meatballs

Hint: *To serve as an entrée, heat in tomato sauce and serve over rice or orzo.*

Salmon Crescents or Strudel

Dough:

3 C flour
Dash salt

1 C butter or margarine
5 to 6 T orange juice

Mix flour and salt together. Cut in butter or margarine until pea-size pieces are formed. Add orange juice, a little at a time, mixing just until the dough forms a ball. Wrap the dough in plastic wrap and chill for at least 30 minutes, or up to a few days.

Filling:

6 to $6\frac{1}{2}$ oz can salmon, drained or
   fresh salmon, cooked and drained
$\frac{1}{2}$ C mayonnaise
1 T lemon juice

1 to $1\frac{1}{2}$ tsp white horseradish
1 T onion, minced
1 egg, beaten with 1 tsp water

To Make Crescents:

Combine all filling ingredients except egg mixture. Roll out dough into (2) 8- or 9-inch circles. Spread half the salmon on 1 circle of dough. Cut the circle into 12 pie-shaped wedges. Roll up each wedge, outside edge to center. Repeat with remaining dough and filling. Place seam-side down on greased cookie sheets. Brush with egg mixture. Bake at 400° for 15 minutes, or until golden.

Yield: 24 crescents

To Make Strudel:

Cut dough into 2 pieces. Roll out each piece into a rectangle about 7"x11" and spread surface with half of the filling mixture to within 1 inch of the outside edges of dough. Roll up jellyroll fashion, sealing edges with water. Place rolls, seam-side down, onto a greased cookie sheet. Brush with egg mixture. Bake at 350° for 25 minutes. Cool slightly and slice into 1-inch pieces.

Yield: 24 strudel pieces

Hint: *These freeze well. To reheat, do not defrost. Bake at 350° for about 10 minutes, or until hot.*

Sausage Cheese Balls

1 lb bulk sausage (pork,
  chicken or turkey)
$\frac{1}{2}$ lb Cheddar cheese

3 C all-purpose baking mix (i.e. Bisquick)
1 egg
$\frac{1}{2}$ to 1 tsp cayenne pepper

Combine all ingredients in a food processor or in a mixing bowl using your hands. Roll the mixture into balls about 1 inch in diameter. Place these on a greased cookie sheet and bake at 375° for 16 to 20 minutes, turning them over after 9 or 10 minutes. Drain on paper towels if necessary. These freeze well. There are 2 ways to freeze. One is to cook the sausage balls completely, cool and freeze. When you want to serve them, do not defrost. Bake in a preheated 350° oven for about 10 minutes, or until hot. The other way is to flash freeze the uncooked sausage balls and then put them in freezer bags. When ready to serve, place in a preheated 350° oven for 10 minutes on 1 side, turn over and cook on the other side for about 8 to 10 minutes, or until hot.

Hint: *If you cannot get bulk sausage, remove sausage meat from its casing and proceed with the recipe. If you don't have any all-purpose baking mix, substitute 3 cups flour and 4 teaspoons baking powder. These are still very tasty when made with chicken sausage and low fat cheese.*

Crab Nibbles

5 oz jar Old English cheese
$\frac{1}{2}$ C butter or margarine, softened
$1\frac{1}{2}$ tsp mayonnaise
$\frac{1}{2}$ tsp seasoned salt (such as Lawry's)

$\frac{1}{4}$ to $\frac{1}{2}$ tsp garlic powder
6 to 7 oz crabmeat, drained and flaked
8 to 9 English muffins

In an electric mixer or processor, combine all ingredients, except muffins. Cut muffins in half and spread crab mixture on each half. Cut each muffin half into 6 triangles. Bake triangles at 375° for 10 minutes, or until bubbly and hot. Broil for 1 to 2 minutes if you like them crispy. If you want to freeze these, put the triangles on a cookie sheet and freeze. Once frozen, put them in freezer bags and freeze until needed. When serving, do not defrost, remove from freezer and bake as above.

Yield: 100 nibbles

Hint: *This hors d'oeuvre takes only about 20 minutes to make. Langostino may be substituted for the crab.*

■ ■

Mini-Herbed Cream Puffs

6 T butter or margarine
1 C water
Dash salt
1 C flour

4 eggs
$\frac{1}{2}$ C Swiss or Parmesan cheese,
  finely grated
$\frac{1}{4}$ tsp dry mustard

In a medium saucepan heat water, butter or margarine and salt over medium heat until boiling. Remove from heat. Beat flour into this mixture until the dough forms a ball. Beat in eggs, 1 at a time, until well mixed. Stir in remaining ingredients. Drop by teaspoonfuls 1 inch apart onto greased cookie sheets. Bake at 425° for 12 to 14 minutes, or until golden. Serve hot or make small canapés by splitting the cooled puffs in half and filling with chicken, tuna, egg or seafood salad.

Yield: $4\frac{1}{2}$ dozen puffs

Hint: *You can make more attractive puffs by using a pastry bag. Use the large round or star tip. The puffs can be frozen. To serve, defrost puffs and bake at 250° for 7 to 10 minutes, or until somewhat crisp.*

Pepperoni Puffs

1 C flour
1 tsp baking powder
1 C milk

1 egg
$\frac{1}{2}$ C Cheddar cheese, shredded
1 C pepperoni, finely diced

Combine all ingredients, except pepperoni. Add pepperoni and blend well so as to evenly distribute. Let batter stand for 10 minutes. Grease or spray 36 mini-muffin pans and pour pepperoni mixture into them. Bake at 350° for 20 to 25 minutes, or until golden.

Yield: 36 puffs

Hint: *You can dice the pepperoni in a food processor, using the steel blade. Also, these may be frozen. To reheat, place frozen puffs on a cookie sheet and bake at 350° for 8 to 10 minutes, or until hot.*

■ ■

Glazed Chicken Wings

3 lbs chicken wings
4 cloves garlic, minced
1 piece ginger (1"x1½"), minced

½ C soy sauce
½ C red wine vinegar
2 C dark brown sugar

Cut off outer tips of wings and discard. Then cut each wing in half. Place wings on a broiler pan and bake at 350° for about 45 minutes, turning once. Then broil for a few minutes, or until wings are golden on each side. While wings are cooking, make the sauce by combining all remaining ingredients. Cook in a large saucepan for 5 minutes. Add cooked wings to the sauce and stir until they are well coated with the sauce.

Hint: *These are wonderful to serve at a party. Keep wings hot in a chafing dish. The food processor is very helpful for finely mincing the garlic and ginger. With the steel blade in place, turn the processor on and then drop the garlic and ginger down the feed tube. This method enables small amounts of food to get more finely minced than if they are just placed in the processor before it is turned on.*

Chinese Chicken Wings

24 chicken wings, cut in half,
  tips removed
3 T ginger, finely minced or grated

3 T hoisin sauce
3 T dry mustard
3 T dry sherry

In a food processor, using the steel blade, combine all the ingredients except the wings. Place wings in a large pan or bowl and pour the mixture over them. Mix well. Marinate for several hours or overnight. To cook, place wings on foil-lined cookie sheets that have been greased or sprayed with nonstick spray. Do not crowd the wings. Bake at 350° for 50 to 60 minutes, turning occasionally. If you want the wings crispy, put them under the broiler for the last few minutes.

Hint: *The food processor makes it really easy to chop the ginger. This marinade is also good with spareribs, pork strips or other chicken parts.*

Broiled Chicken Fingers

2 lbs skinless and boneless
  chicken breasts
$\frac{1}{2}$ C bread crumbs
$\frac{1}{2}$ C Parmesan cheese, grated

1 tsp rosemary
Salt and black pepper, to taste
1 to 2 T olive oil or 1 egg white, beaten
Lemon wedges, for garnish

Cut the breasts into thick strips. On a plate or wax paper, combine the bread crumbs, cheese, rosemary, salt and pepper. Brush oil on the chicken strips or dip them in egg white. Then dip them into the crumb mixture, making sure to coat both sides. Spray a cookie sheet with nonstick spray and place chicken pieces on it. Place cookie sheet close to the broiler element and broil for 2 to 3 minutes, or until golden on 1 side. Turn over and broil until second side is golden. Serve hot, squeezing lemon juice over chicken, if desired.

Hint: *This tasty hors d'oeuvre is a low fat version of the popular chicken fingers served in restaurants. Feel free to season the bread crumbs with whichever spices you prefer.*

Tiny Herb Toasts

$\frac{1}{3}$ C butter or margarine
$\frac{1}{4}$ tsp oregano
$\frac{1}{4}$ tsp basil
$\frac{1}{4}$ tsp thyme

$\frac{1}{4}$ tsp rosemary
3 T parsley, minced
12 slices thin white or
  whole wheat bread

Cream butter or margarine with all the seasonings and blend well. Trim crusts from bread and spread each piece with herb mixture. Cut each piece into 4 squares. Place on cookie sheets and bake at 250° for 1 hour. Cool and place in a tin or other airtight container where they can be kept at room temperature for up to a week or frozen for up to 2 months. Serve at room temperature.

Hint: *These can also be used as a snack or as a garnish for soup or salad. You can purchase "tiny toast crackers" and use those instead of bread.*

Stuffed Mushrooms

24 mushrooms
$\frac{1}{2}$ stalk celery, finely minced
1 small onion, finely minced
2 garlic cloves, finely minced or
   garlic powder, to taste

1 T butter or margarine
$\frac{1}{4}$ C dry white wine or vermouth
$\frac{1}{3}$ C seasoned bread crumbs
2 T Parmesan cheese, grated

Remove stems from mushrooms and finely chop. Sauté stems, celery, onion and garlic in butter or margarine until tender. Add wine and simmer for 5 minutes. Stir in bread crumbs. Place mixture in mushroom caps and sprinkle with Parmesan cheese. Place on a greased cookie sheet or ovenproof dish and bake at 350° for 10 to 15 minutes, or until cheese is melted and mushrooms are hot.

Yield: 24 stuffed mushrooms

Crab-Stuffed Mushrooms

30 mushrooms
2 T butter or margarine
1 medium onion, finely chopped
$\frac{1}{2}$ C Ritz or cheese crackers, crushed
2 T dry sherry

6 oz crabmeat or surimi (imitation
   crab), finely shredded
$\frac{1}{4}$ C Monterey Jack cheese,
   shredded (optional)
Salt and pepper, to taste

Remove stems from mushrooms and chop. Melt butter or margarine in a fry pan. Add onions and chopped stems. Sauté until tender. Combine remaining ingredients and fold in mushroom stem mixture. Spoon mixture into mushroom caps. Place on a greased cookie sheet and bake at 350° for 10 to 12 minutes, or until tender.

Yield: 30 stuffed mushrooms

Hint: *You can use a food processor to chop all the ingredients finely.*

■ ■ ■■ ■

Hot Crab and Artichoke Dip

$13\frac{3}{4}$ oz can water-packed artichoke hearts
6 to 8 oz crab meat or imitation
  crab (surimi)
$\frac{3}{4}$ C mayonnaise
1 C mild salsa

2 T white wine or dry vermouth
1 C Parmesan cheese, freshly
  grated, divided
Crackers, French bread or pita bread

Squeeze, drain and chop artichokes. Flake crab. Combine these in a bowl and add mayonnaise, salsa, wine and $\frac{3}{4}$ cup of the Parmesan. Blend well. Pour into an ovenproof casserole and sprinkle with remaining $\frac{1}{4}$ cup cheese. Bake at 375° for 15 minutes, or until golden and bubbly. Serve with French bread or pita bread.

Hot Artichoke and Spinach Dip

$13\frac{3}{4}$ oz can water-packed artichokes,
  drained and minced
5 to 6 oz frozen chopped
  spinach, thawed and drained
1 C Parmesan cheese, grated

1 C mayonnaise
2 cloves garlic, minced
Black pepper, to taste
1 tomato, chopped, for garnish
1 to 2 scallions, chopped, for garnish

Combine all ingredients except tomatoes and scallions. Pour into a 9-inch pie plate or casserole dish and bake at 350° for 20 minutes. Sprinkle chopped tomatoes and scallions on top. Serve with pita bread triangles or nacho chips.

Hint: *The dip can be made several hours in advance. Heat right before serving.*

Guacamole

1 very ripe avocado
$\frac{1}{2}$ tsp lemon juice
1 medium tomato, finely diced

$\frac{1}{2}$ tsp chili powder, or to taste
1 clove garlic, minced
Salt and pepper, to taste

Peel avocado and mash well with a fork. Add remaining ingredients, blending well. Serve with nacho chips or crackers.

Hint: *When peeling and cutting the avocado, save the pit. When you have mixed everything together, place the pit in the dip because this helps to prevent the avocado from discoloring. Remove pit before serving.*

Roasted Peppers on Bruschetta

4 yellow, orange, red or green
  peppers, or combination
1 to 2 T olive oil
2 T balsamic vinegar
2 cloves garlic, minced

Salt and pepper, to taste
2 tsp capers (optional)
1 to 2 tsp olive oil (for bread)
12 to 15 slices Italian bread
  (day-old is best)

Place peppers on a broiler pan or on a grill as close to the broiling element as possible. Broil or grill, turning several times so that peppers are charred all over. Place the peppers in a brown paper or plastic bag for at least 10 minutes. Remove from the bag and cut in half. Discard seeds and peel. Cut peppers into thin strips and place in a bowl. Add just enough oil to moisten them. Add balsamic vinegar, garlic, salt, pepper and capers, if desired. Stir mixture. Cover and marinate in the refrigerator for a few hours or up to a few days before serving. To serve, place the bread on a cookie sheet and brush each slice with a little olive oil. Bake at 400° for 5 minutes, or until lightly golden. Place some pepper strips on each piece of bread.

Curry Dip

1 pt mayonnaise
1 T curry powder
$\frac{1}{4}$ tsp pepper
1 T onion, finely minced

3 T chili sauce
$\frac{1}{4}$ tsp salt
1 T garlic powder
1 T Worcestershire sauce

Combine all ingredients and chill. Serve with crudités (raw vegetables) or crackers.

Hint: *This will keep well in the refrigerator for a few weeks.*

Hummus

2 to 3 cloves garlic, minced
15 to 19 oz can chickpeas,
  drained and rinsed
$\frac{1}{4}$ C olive oil

$\frac{1}{4}$ to $\frac{1}{3}$ C fresh lemon juice, or to taste
3 to 4 T sesame tahini, or to taste
Salt and pepper, to taste

Place garlic in a food processor or blender and chop finely. Add remaining ingredients, seasoning to taste. Chill for at least several hours before serving. Serve with pita bread or crudités (raw vegetables).

Mushroom Almond Paté

$\frac{3}{4}$ C slivered almonds
1 to 2 tsp butter or margarine
$\frac{3}{4}$ lb mushrooms, sliced
1 small onion, diced
2 cloves garlic, minced

$\frac{1}{4}$ tsp thyme
$\frac{1}{2}$ tsp salt, or to taste
$\frac{1}{8}$ tsp white pepper, or to taste
1 tsp canola or olive oil

Toast almonds at 350° for 5 to 10 minutes, or until golden. Set aside. Melt butter or margarine in a fry pan and add everything except oil and almonds. Cook, stirring occasionally until mushrooms and onions are soft or until most of the liquid evaporates, approximately 10 to 15 minutes. With the steel blade of a food processor, coarsely chop 2 tablespoons of the toasted almonds and reserve. Chop remaining almonds until finely ground. Add mushroom mixture and oil to processor and fold in reserved chopped almonds. Serve at room temperature with crackers or raw vegetables. If made ahead, cool, cover and chill.

Hint: To clean mushrooms, do not soak them because they will absorb the water and when cooked they will exude the water which will dilute their flavor. Rather, brush mushrooms with a mushroom brush or other soft brush to get off excess dirt. Rinse the brush with water and shake off the excess and then clean a few mushrooms. Repeat until all the mushrooms are clean.

Cannellini Bean Dip or Sandwich Paté

1 T olive oil
1 large onion, chopped
3 cloves garlic, minced
(2) 15 to 19 oz cans cannellini
  (white kidney) beans,
  well rinsed and drained

2 T white wine vinegar
$\frac{1}{2}$ to 1 tsp cumin
$\frac{1}{2}$ to 1 tsp coriander
$\frac{1}{2}$ tsp allspice
Salt and pepper, to taste

Heat oil in a fry pan and add onion. Cook over low-medium heat for 10 minutes, or until onion is soft, but not brown. Add garlic and cook for 1 additional minute. Transfer cooked mixture to a food processor. Add beans, vinegar and spices and purée until smooth. Taste to adjust seasonings. Chill for a few hours to blend flavors. Serve as a dip with pita bread triangles, crackers or vegetables. You can also use as a filling for sandwiches by spreading some paté on pita bread, along with some alfalfa sprouts and/or sliced tomatoes

Hint: This recipe is low in fat and delicious as both a dip or sandwich filling.

Black Bean Dip

2 cloves garlic
$\frac{1}{4}$ medium onion
15 oz can black beans, drained
   and rinsed

2 T lime juice
2 T orange juice
Salt and pepper, to taste

With the motor of the food processor running, drop garlic and onion down the feed tube and process until finely minced. Add remaining ingredients, processing until smooth. Serve with tortilla chips or crudités (raw vegetables).

Hint: *You can use a blender instead of a processor. This mixture can be used as a filling for quesadillas and served as a snack or lunch.*

Mexican Black Bean Dip

(2) 19 oz cans black beans, rinsed and
   well drained
1 C red onion, finely chopped
1 C corn, canned or frozen, drained

1 C medium or hot salsa
1 C red pepper, chopped
1 C Cheddar cheese, grated
1 C sour cream

In a large bowl, combine all ingredients and mix well. Allow to sit for at least 1 hour, or up to a day ahead, before serving. Serve with nacho chips or pita bread triangles.

Hint: *To reduce fat, use low fat sour cream and low fat Cheddar cheese.*

Kidney Bean Dip

(2) 16 oz cans kidney beans
$1\frac{1}{3}$ C hot red pepper relish
3 to 4 tsp horseradish, or to taste

$\frac{2}{3}$ C mayonnaise
Garlic powder, to taste
3 drops Tabasco sauce, or to taste

Rinse kidney beans and drain well. Combine remaining ingredients, then add kidney beans. Fold together carefully so that beans will not get mashed. Chill for several hours before serving. Serve with nacho chips.

Hint: *This dip will keep well in the refrigerator for a few days. However, the spicy flavor weakens as it ages. If you like it spicier, add more Tabasco. You can use low fat mayonnaise to make this a healthy dip.*

Pesto Cheese Spread

8 oz cream cheese, softened $\frac{1}{3}$ to $\frac{1}{2}$ C pesto sauce

Using an electric mixer or food processor, thoroughly blend pesto and cheese together. Serve as a spread for crackers or crudités (raw vegetables). You can also thinly spread it on slices of ham or roast beef and roll them up and cut into $\frac{3}{4}$-inch slices. Turn on end to resemble pinwheels.

Hint: Pesto spread is also delicious used in place of mayonnaise on roast beef or turkey sandwiches.

Cranberry Pesto

1 C cranberries
5 basil leaves (fresh or frozen)
2 T lemon juice
1 to 3 T sugar, divided

Salt and pepper, to taste
3 to 4 T olive oil
$\frac{1}{2}$ C walnuts

Place cranberries, basil, lemon juice, 1 tablespoon of the sugar and salt and pepper in a food processor. Add nuts and oil. Using the steel blade, process to a coarse textured spread. Add remaining sugar, to taste. Cover and refrigerate. Spread a thin layer on crackers or sliced French bread. Top with thinly sliced turkey breast or Brie cheese.

Hint: If you want to use this pesto on pasta, use only 1 tablespoon sugar.

Delicious Dilly Dip

1 medium white or red onion,
   finely chopped
1 C mayonnaise

1 C sour cream
$\frac{3}{4}$ C fresh dill, chopped
1 round pumpernickel bread

Combine all the ingredients except the bread. Slice the top off the bread. Using a grapefruit knife, cut a big hole deep enough into the center of the bread to hold the dip. Cut the scooped-out bread into cubes and arrange them, along with some sliced fresh veggies, around the scooped-out bread. Fill the hole in the bread with the dip.

Hint: Low fat mayonnaise and reduced fat sour cream can be used in this recipe with tasty results.

SOUPS

Pumpkin Apple Soup

3 lbs fresh or (2) 16 oz cans pumpkin
6 C chicken or vegetable broth
2 Granny Smith apples,
  peeled and cubed
1 large onion, chopped
$\frac{1}{2}$ tsp rosemary

1 tsp thyme
$\frac{1}{2}$ C milk or half and half
Salt and pepper, to taste
$\frac{1}{2}$ C sour cream or yogurt, for garnish
Croutons, for garnish

Peel and cube pumpkin and cut into 2-inch pieces. Heat broth in a large pot. Add pumpkin, apples, onion and spices. Bring to a boil, reduce to a simmer, cover and cook for 30 minutes, or until apples and vegetables are tender. Purée in a food processor or blender. Return soup to the pan and add milk or half and half and simmer for 5 minutes. Season with salt and pepper, to taste. Serve with a dollop of sour cream or yogurt and croutons, if desired.

Hint: *If using fresh pumpkin, to avoid the drudgery of peeling and cutting it, wash it and poke it all over with the tines of a roasting fork. Place on a plate, uncovered, in the microwave and cook on high for 10 minutes. Turn over and cook for another 10 minutes. Remove from microwave and cool briefly. Cut open, remove and discard the seeds (or roast, if desired). Using a spoon, scrape flesh of pumpkin from the skin and place in the soup pot and proceed with recipe.*

Tortellini and Bean Soup

1 tsp olive oil
3 cloves garlic, minced
1 medium onion, diced
40 to 44 oz chicken or
  vegetable broth
14½ oz can stewed tomatoes
2 C raw spinach or 10 oz pkg frozen
  chopped spinach, thawed and drained

1 tsp oregano
1 tsp basil
Black pepper, to taste
12 oz fresh or frozen cheese tortellini
15½ oz can kidney beans,
  rinsed and drained
Parmesan cheese, for garnish

Heat oil in a large pot and add garlic and onion. Cook for about 2 minutes, or until it begins to get golden in color. Add chicken broth and bring to a boil. Break up tomatoes with a fork or potato masher and add to soup. Add the spinach, spices, tortellini and kidney beans and bring to a boil. Reduce heat and simmer for 10 to 15 minutes. Sprinkle with grated Parmesan cheese, if desired.

Hint: *This is a quick and nutritious meal made in only 1 pot.*

Vegetable Bean Soup

15 to 19 oz can kidney beans
15 to 19 oz can cannellini (white
  kidney) beans
3 carrots, diced
4 celery stalks, diced
2 large onions, diced

1½ to 2 T Worcestershire sauce
6 oz tomato paste
1 bay leaf
¼ tsp marjoram
Black pepper, to taste
4 to 4½ C water

Rinse and drain the beans. Combine all ingredients in a large pot. Bring to a boil, reduce heat and simmer for 1 hour. Discard bay leaf before serving.

Hint: *Because this soup has Worcestershire sauce and water as a base, it is much lower in sodium than many similar soups which contain commercial stock or broth.*

Chicken or Turkey Minestrone Soup

1 tsp olive oil
1 large onion, chopped
4 carrots, sliced
2 stalks celery, sliced
2 bay leaves
1 to $1\frac{1}{2}$ lbs skinless and boneless
  chicken or turkey breast
7 C chicken broth

15 to 19 oz can cannellini (white kidney)
  beans, rinsed and drained
1 C fresh or defrosted frozen peas
$14\frac{1}{2}$ oz can tomatoes, undrained
  and chopped
2 to 3 T chopped parsley
  or basil, for garnish
Freshly grated Parmesan cheese, for garnish

Heat oil in a large pot. Add onion, carrots, celery and bay leaves and cook for about 5 minutes. Add the chicken or turkey and broth and bring to a boil. Reduce heat to low and simmer for 5 minutes. Transfer chicken or turkey to a plate and when it is cool enough to handle, cut it into bite-size pieces. Add beans and tomatoes to the broth and cook for about 30 minutes. Just before serving, add the peas and chicken or turkey and cook just until hot. Garnish with basil or parsley and Parmesan cheese.

Hint: *If you prefer, use 2 to 3 fresh tomatoes rather than canned. This quick and easy soup tastes like chicken or turkey soup that took all day to prepare!*

Minestrone Soup With Beef

1 T olive oil
1 lb ground beef
1 large onion, chopped
3 garlic cloves, minced
1 medium eggplant, peeled and cubed
2 carrots, chopped
2 stalks celery, chopped
5 C beef broth

28 oz can crushed Italian tomatoes
$\frac{1}{2}$ tsp nutmeg
2 T parsley, chopped
$\frac{1}{2}$ C small pasta (tiny shells,
  stars, orzo, etc.)
Salt and pepper, to taste
Grated Parmesan cheese, for garnish

Heat oil in a large soup pot and add ground beef, onion and garlic. Cook until meat is no longer pink. Add eggplant, carrots, celery, broth, tomatoes, nutmeg and parsley. Bring to a boil, reduce heat, and simmer over low heat for 30 minutes. Add pasta and simmer for an additional 30 minutes. Season with salt and pepper. Garnish with Parmesan cheese, if desired.

Hint: *This soup freezes well. You can substitute ground turkey or chicken for the beef.*

■ ● ■ ● ■ ● ■ ■ ● ■ ● ■ ■ ● ■ ● ■ ● ■ ● ■ ● ■ ● ■ ■ ● ■ ● ■ ● ■ ■ ■

Cheddar Cheese Soup

1 T butter or margarine
$\frac{1}{2}$ C carrots, chopped
$\frac{1}{2}$ C onion, chopped
$\frac{3}{4}$ C fresh dill, chopped
$\frac{1}{2}$ C celery, chopped
6 T flour

5 C chicken or vegetable broth
2 C sharp Cheddar cheese, grated or
   cut into small cubes
2 C half and half or milk
Salt and white pepper, to taste
2 T sesame seeds, toasted, for garnish

Melt butter or margarine in a large saucepan. Add carrots, onion, dill and celery and sauté until tender. Sprinkle in flour, 1 tablespoon at a time, stirring after each addition. Add the broth. Bring to a boil and cook for about 5 minutes. Using a slotted spoon, strain out the vegetables and purée them in a food processor. Return purée to the soup in the saucepan and cook over medium heat just until the soup boils. Then reduce heat and simmer for 15 to 20 minutes. Add the cheese, whisking constantly until the cheese is melted. Slowly add the half and half or milk and stir until blended. Season with salt and pepper, to taste. Garnish with toasted sesame seeds.

Tomato Soup

Featured in Cover Photo

2 tsp olive or canola oil
4 scallions, chopped
4 cloves garlic, finely minced
$\frac{1}{2}$ C (4 oz jar) pimento (roasted
   sweet red peppers), drained
$3\frac{1}{2}$ C chicken or vegetable
   broth, divided
3 T basil, finely chopped or 1 T dried

28 oz can crushed tomatoes in
   tomato purée
3 T (1 T dried) parsley
$14\frac{1}{2}$ oz can whole tomatoes
$\frac{1}{2}$ C orzo or other small pasta
Salt and pepper, to taste
Parmesan cheese, grated (optional)

Heat oil in a large pot. Add scallions and cook for about 5 minutes, or until tender. Add garlic and cook for 1 minute. Purée pimentos in a blender or food processor with 1 cup of the broth. Add puréed mixture, along with remaining broth, crushed tomatoes, basil and parsley to the pot. Drain the juice from whole tomatoes into the pot. Coarsely chop the tomatoes and add them. Add orzo and simmer over low heat for 10 to 15 minutes, or until pasta is al dente. Garnish with fresh Parmesan cheese, if desired.

Hint: *This hearty soup is easy to make, low in fat, and uses ingredients you probably have on hand throughout the year. The ratio of fresh herbs to dried is 3:1. In other words, 1 tablespoon fresh herbs equals 1 teaspoon dried.*

Clam Chowder

(1 or 2) 10 oz cans whole baby clams
(2) 6 oz cans minced clams
3 to 4 T butter or margarine
3 medium onions, finely chopped
1 clove garlic, finely minced

2 large potatoes, cut into $\frac{1}{2}$" cubes
8 oz bottle clam juice
1 pt half and half or milk
Salt and white pepper, to taste

Drain the clams and reserve the juice. Melt the butter or margarine in a large pot. Add the onion and garlic and sauté until very soft. Add the potatoes, reserved clam juice and bottled clam juice. Simmer until potatoes are almost tender, approximately 20 to 25 minutes. Add clams, half and half or milk and salt and pepper. Simmer over low heat for 5 to 10 minutes.

Hint: For an extra delicious taste, use fresh chopped clams instead of canned. You'll be amazed at how delicious and authentic tasting this chowder is even though it doesn't contain any bacon or pork. When made with 1% milk it is rich tasting, while low in fat.

Avgolemo Soup
(Greek Egg Lemon Soup)

6 C chicken broth
Rind of 1 lemon, grated
$\frac{3}{4}$ C rice or orzo

Juice of 1 lemon
2 eggs
Salt, to taste

Bring the broth to a boil and add lemon rind. Add rice or orzo and simmer just until al dente, about 15 minutes for the rice, 5 to 6 minutes for the orzo. Whisk lemon juice and eggs together. Pour 1 cup of the boiling broth into the egg mixture and blend well. Pour egg mixture into the broth. Stir to blend, but do not boil. Add salt, to taste.

Hint: Small pieces of chicken may be added to the soup. You can use low sodium chicken broth and egg substitute, if desired.

Black Bean Soup

12 oz dried black beans
8 C chicken or vegetable broth
2 tsp olive oil
1 onion, chopped
2 carrots, chopped
2 stalks celery, chopped
2 cloves garlic, minced

2 tsp oregano
1 tsp thyme
1 bay leaf
$\frac{1}{2}$ tsp cayenne pepper
3 T lime juice
Salt and pepper, to taste
Fresh cilantro, for garnish (optional)

Rinse and sort beans, discarding any that are shriveled. Place beans in a large soup pot and cover with water. Soak for 8 hours or overnight. Drain beans and return to pot. In a large skillet, heat olive oil and add onion, carrots, celery and garlic and sauté for about 5 minutes, or until onion and garlic are tender. Transfer this mixture to the soup pot and add oregano, thyme, bay leaf and cayenne pepper. Bring mixture to a boil. Cover and reduce heat to a simmer and cook for $3\frac{1}{2}$ to 4 hours, or until beans are tender. Cool soup slightly and remove and discard bay leaf. Transfer soup, in batches, to a food processor or blender and purée to desired thickness. Add lime juice and salt and pepper, to taste. If desired, garnish with cilantro.

Hint: *When I hear that a snowstorm or cold snap is predicted, I start soaking my beans and get ready to make soup. A snow day to me is a "bread and soup day"!*

Indian Pea Soup in the Crock Pot

1 lb yellow or green split peas
2 celery stalks, finely chopped
1 carrot, finely chopped
1 medium onion, finely chopped
2 T butter or margarine
2 to 3 tsp curry powder

1 T lemon juice
1 bay leaf
3 chicken or vegetarian bouillon cubes
2 qts water
$\frac{1}{2}$ tsp salt, or to taste

Combine all ingredients in a crock pot. Stir, cover and cook on high for 6 to 7 hours or on low for 9 hours, or until everything is tender.

■ ■

Cream of Mushroom Soup

2 T butter or margarine, divided
1 lb mushrooms, sliced
$\frac{3}{4}$ C celery, chopped (2 stalks)
$\frac{1}{3}$ C onion, chopped ($\frac{1}{4}$ medium onion)
3 C chicken or vegetable broth

3 T flour
1$\frac{1}{3}$ C milk or cream
Salt and pepper, to taste
2 T dry white wine (optional)

Melt 1 tablespoon butter or margarine in a large pot. Add mushrooms and cook for 2 to 3 minutes. Add celery, onion and broth. Bring to a boil. Reduce heat and simmer for 30 to 35 minutes, or until vegetables are soft. Transfer vegetable mixture to a food processor or blender and purée. Pour into a large bowl and set aside. Heat 1 tablespoon butter or margarine in the original pot until melted. Whisk in flour and cook for 1 to 2 minutes. Slowly add milk or cream and keep stirring until mixture almost comes to a boil. Cook for 1 additional minute and remove from heat. Stir in mushroom purée and add salt and pepper, to taste. Add wine, if desired. Return to low heat and heat gently, but do not boil.

Hint: *This is a delicious soup that is easy to make. As a low fat alternative, use low fat milk instead of cream.*

Lentil and Brown Rice Soup

6 C chicken or vegetable broth
4 C water
1$\frac{1}{2}$ C lentils, picked over and rinsed
1 C long-grain brown rice
35 oz can tomatoes, drained (save the juice) and chopped
3 carrots, chopped
1 large onion, chopped
1 large stalk celery, chopped

3 large cloves garlic (1 T), minced
$\frac{1}{2}$ tsp basil
$\frac{1}{2}$ tsp oregano
$\frac{1}{2}$ tsp thyme
1 bay leaf
$\frac{1}{2}$ C parsley, minced
2 T cider vinegar, or to taste
Salt and freshly ground pepper, to taste

In a large, heavy saucepan or large pot, combine the broth, water, lentils, rice, tomatoes, reserved tomato juice, carrots, onion, celery, garlic, basil, oregano, thyme and bay leaf. Bring the soup to a boil. Reduce heat. Cover pan and simmer the soup, stirring occasionally, for 45 to 55 minutes, or until the lentils and rice are both tender. Remove from heat and discard the bay leaf. Stir in the parsley, vinegar, salt and pepper. If soup becomes too thick, thin it with additional hot broth or water.

Hint: *This soup is high in fiber and flavor!*

Mediterranean Onion Soup

5 C onions, thinly sliced
I tsp salt
I tsp sugar
$\frac{1}{4}$ tsp pepper
3 T olive oil
3 garlic cloves, crushed
I parsley sprig
I tsp thyme

$\frac{3}{4}$ tsp oregano
I bay leaf
35 oz can Italian tomatoes
I T tomato paste
5 C chicken stock
$\frac{1}{4}$ C small pasta
Grated Parmesan or Gruyere
   cheese, for garnish

In a large pot, sauté the onions, salt, sugar and pepper in the oil until the onions are pale golden, about 15 minutes. Partially cover and cook until they are very soft and browned. Stir in the garlic, parsley, thyme, oregano and bay leaf. Cook for 2 minutes. Drain the tomatoes and purée in a food processor or blender. Stir puréed tomatoes into the onions and add the tomato paste and stock. Simmer, partially covered, for 30 minutes. Adjust the seasoning with salt and pepper. Add the pasta and simmer, uncovered, until tender. Discard the bay leaf and parsley. Garnish with grated cheese, if desired.

Hint: *This can be made ahead and refrigerated or frozen.*

Cold Blueberry Soup

2 C blueberries
I C water
$\frac{1}{2}$ C sugar
$\frac{1}{2}$ C lemon juice
I tsp cinnamon

I C yogurt
I C sour cream
$\frac{1}{2}$ to $\frac{2}{3}$ C dry red or blush wine
$\frac{2}{3}$ C blueberries, for garnish

Purée berries in a blender or food processor until smooth. In a saucepan combine puréed berries, water, sugar, lemon juice and cinnamon. Cover and bring to a boil. Immediately turn down heat and simmer for 10 minutes. Whisk in remaining ingredients, blending until smooth. Chill for several hours or overnight before serving. To serve, pour into chilled soup bowls or mugs and sprinkle with a few fresh berries.

Yield: 4 cups soup

Hint: *For optimum taste, make this a day in advance. If fresh blueberries are not available, you can use frozen unthawed berries. Also, raspberries may be substituted for the blueberries. You can substitute low fat sour cream for regular sour cream.*

SALADS AND JELLO MOLDS

Crunchy Chinese Cabbage Salad

Salad:

1 head (1 lb) Chinese cabbage, coarsely chopped

4 scallions, sliced

Crunchy Mixture:

$1\frac{1}{2}$ T butter or margarine
$\frac{1}{4}$ C sesame seeds
1 T sugar
$\frac{1}{3}$ C slivered almonds

1 pkg Chinese Ramen noodles (noodles only from 3 oz pkg of noodle soup), crushed, or $\frac{1}{2}$ C fine egg noodles, crushed

Dressing:

$\frac{1}{4}$ C canola oil
$\frac{1}{4}$ C water
3 T red wine vinegar

$\frac{1}{3}$ C sugar
$1\frac{1}{2}$ T soy sauce

To make crunchy mixture, sauté all crunchy ingredients in a large skillet over low to medium heat until golden colored. Stir often to prevent burning. Cool and set aside. Shake dressing ingredients in a jar. Place cabbage and scallions in a large bowl. Sprinkle with crunchy mixture. Pour dressing over salad and toss well.

Hint: *The dressing can be made several days in advance and kept in the refrigerator. The crunchy mixture may also be made ahead and kept in a tin or other tightly sealed container. Assemble just before serving. Regular green cabbage can be substituted for Chinese cabbage.*

Egg-Free Caesar Salad

Dressing:

1 T red wine vinegar
1 T anchovies, minced or
  anchovy paste (optional)
1 T Dijon mustard
4 cloves garlic, minced

$\frac{1}{2}$ tsp black pepper, or to taste
1 C olive oil
4 T lemon juice (1 lemon)
Dash Worcestershire sauce
Salt, to taste

Place all the ingredients in a jar and cover tightly. Shake vigorously until well blended. Refrigerate for a minimum of several hours or up to 1 week.

Salad:

2 heads Romaine lettuce
$\frac{3}{4}$ to 1 C freshly grated Parmesan cheese

2 C croutons

Wash lettuce and tear into bite-size pieces. Dry lettuce thoroughly. Place lettuce in a large bowl. Just before serving, sprinkle with cheese and croutons and add dressing. Toss well.

Hint: *To reduce fat and calories, you can substitute water for half the oil without sacrificing too much flavor. The lettuce can be washed and dried up to 2 days in advance. To keep the lettuce crisp, dry it in a salad spinner and then wrap it in a few paper towels and place it in a large plastic bag.*

Carrot Salad

$3\frac{1}{2}$ C (10 oz pkg) carrots, shredded
1 to 2 T canola oil
2 T lemon juice
$1\frac{1}{2}$ to 2 T red wine vinegar

$\frac{1}{2}$ tsp sugar
$\frac{1}{2}$ tsp salt, or to taste
Freshly ground black pepper, to taste

Combine all ingredients in a medium bowl. Cover and refrigerate for at least 2 to 3 hours, or up to 2 days, before serving.

Hint: *When prices for salad greens are high, carrot salad is a good alternative.*

■ ■

Marinated Cole Slaw

Salad:

1 head cabbage, shredded
2 stalks celery, sliced
2 carrots, grated

1 medium onion, chopped
$\frac{1}{2}$ green pepper, chopped

Dressing:

$\frac{2}{3}$ C vinegar
$\frac{1}{3}$ C olive or canola oil
1 tsp dry mustard

1 tsp celery seed
2 to 3 tsp salt
$\frac{1}{2}$ C sugar

Place cabbage and other veggies in a large bowl. Combine dressing ingredients and place in a saucepan over medium heat. Bring to a boil and remove from heat. Cool and pour over cabbage mixture. Refrigerate for at least 8 hours before serving. This will keep in refrigerator for several days.

Hint: *To save time, buy shredded cabbage and shredded carrots at the supermarket.*

Pan-Seared Portobello Salad

Salad:

6 C Romaine, red or green leaf lettuce,
  cleaned and torn into bite-size pieces
$\frac{1}{4}$ large red onion, thinly sliced
$\frac{1}{4}$ C Greek black olives (optional)

$\frac{1}{3}$ to $\frac{1}{2}$ C Feta cheese, crumbled
1 T olive oil
6 oz portobello mushrooms, diced

Dressing:

2 T olive oil, divided
2 T lemon juice

1 clove garlic, minced
Salt and pepper, to taste

Place lettuce, red onion, olives and cheese in a large salad bowl. Combine dressing ingredients in a jar and shake well. Heat olive oil in a fry pan until hot. Add mushrooms and cook, stirring often, for about 3 to 4 minutes, or until golden in color. Cool slightly. Add to salad mixture. Pour dressing on top and toss.

Hint: *The warm mushrooms complement this salad well.*

■ ■

Pasta and Tuna Salad

$\frac{1}{2}$ C olive or canola oil
2 cloves garlic, minced
$\frac{1}{2}$ tsp salt, or to taste
$\frac{1}{2}$ tsp black pepper, or to taste
4 to 5 T red wine vinegar
$1\frac{1}{2}$ tsp oregano

8 oz pasta (3 to $3\frac{1}{2}$ C cooked) such as
  rotini or shells
2 C broccoli florets or
  carrot slices, blanched
1 red or green pepper, cut into cubes
$6\frac{1}{2}$ oz can tuna or salmon

Combine oil, garlic, salt, pepper, oregano and vinegar in a jar. Cover tightly and shake to blend. Cook and drain pasta. While still hot, toss with 3 to 4 tablespoons dressing. Add remaining ingredients and as much of the dressing as needed. Chill for a few hours before serving.

Hint: *This recipe is very versatile because you can substitute poached or grilled chicken, seafood, or beef for the tuna. Also, vary the vegetables to suit your taste or the season.*

Tortellini Salad

14 oz cheese tortellini
$\frac{1}{3}$ C pesto sauce
$\frac{1}{2}$ C roasted red peppers or 1 medium
  red pepper, roasted,
  peeled and sliced
24 pea pods
1 medium green pepper, thinly sliced

$\frac{1}{2}$ C black olives, pitted and
  sliced (optional)
1 C broccoli florets
1 T lemon juice
$\frac{1}{2}$ C Romano cheese, grated
Basil leaves, for garnish (optional)

Bring a large pot of water to a boil and cook tortellini until al dente. Turn off the heat and put pea pods and broccoli in the hot water with the pasta for about 30 seconds, or until bright green. Pour pasta and vegetables into a colander and immediately rinse with cold water. Drain well. Transfer to a large bowl and add remaining ingredients. Mix well. Add more pesto and cheese, if desired. Garnish with fresh basil. Serve at room temperature or cold.

Hint: *You can use roasted red peppers from a jar (pimento) or roast your own red pepper by placing it under the broiler or on a barbecue grill and cooking it until the skin becomes charred. Keep turning the pepper until the entire skin is burnt. Remove from heat and place in a paper or plastic bag for 10 minutes. Remove from the bag. Using a sharp paring knife, peel off skin. Cut pepper open and remove seeds. Cut into thin slices.*

California Tuna Salad

Salad:

1 head, red or green leaf lettuce, washed and dried
(2) 6$\frac{1}{2}$ oz cans tuna, drained
$\frac{1}{2}$ to 1 red onion, sliced

1 avocado, cubed
2 oranges, cubed
2 hard boiled eggs, quartered (optional)
$\frac{1}{4}$ C walnuts, coarsely chopped

Dressing:

$\frac{1}{3}$ to $\frac{1}{2}$ C olive oil
5 T vinegar
4 T sugar
1 T onion, finely chopped

1 tsp prepared mustard
3 T poppy seeds
$\frac{1}{2}$ tsp salt, or to taste
Black pepper, to taste

Tear lettuce into bite-size pieces and place in a large bowl. Place all remaining ingredients, except dressing, on top of lettuce. Mix dressing in a food processor or shake in a covered jar. Pour dressing over salad and toss.

Hint: *This salad is an unusual combination of tastes, textures and colors. It is especially appropriate for brunch or a light luncheon.*

Tuna Salad With a Tang

6$\frac{1}{2}$ oz can white tuna, packed in water
$\frac{1}{4}$ C carrots, grated ($\frac{1}{2}$ large carrot)
$\frac{1}{4}$ C onion, minced (1 small onion)

3 T mayonnaise
1 T lemon juice
1 to 2 tsp sweet relish (optional)

Mash tuna with a fork and add remaining ingredients, mixing until desired consistency is reached, or use a food processor to combine just until blended. Do not overprocess. Adjust seasonings to taste. Serve on bread or bagels with lettuce and sliced tomatoes, if desired.

Hint: *You can make this into a dip by using more mayonnaise and lemon juice.*

■ ■

Pasta Salad With Fat Free Dressing

Salad:

12 oz pasta shells, rotini, etc.
13¾ oz can water-packed artichoke
  hearts, drained and quartered
1 red pepper, diced

1 to 2 C mushrooms, sliced
½ C sun dried tomatoes,
  chopped (optional)

Dressing:

1 C cider vinegar
⅓ C rice vinegar
2 T lemon juice
2 tsp Dijon or Pommery mustard
2 scallions, chopped

1 clove garlic, minced
1 tsp basil
½ tsp oregano
3 T water
Salt and pepper, to taste

Boil pasta until al dente. Drain and transfer to a large bowl. Add artichoke hearts, red pepper, mushrooms and sun dried tomatoes. In a jar, combine ingredients for dressing and shake until well blended. Pour over pasta and veggies and mix well. Refrigerate until serving time.

Hint: *This salad is so delicious that you would never guess that there is no oil in the dressing.*

Lebanese Salad

Salad:

1 head Romaine, green leaf or red leaf,
  lettuce torn into bite-size pieces
1 cucumber, sliced

2 to 3 tomatoes, cubed
¼ C parsley, minced
¼ C mint, minced

Dressing:

¼ C olive or canola oil
¼ C fresh lemon juice
1 tsp salt, or to taste

1 clove garlic, minced
Black pepper, to taste

Combine salad ingredients in a large salad bowl. Combine dressing ingredients in a jar and shake well. Refrigerate. Pour dressing on top and toss well.

■ ■

Chicken or Turkey, Apple and Walnut Salad

2 apples, cored and chopped (leave skin on)
1½ tsp lemon juice
4 to 5 C cooked chicken or turkey breast, cut into ½" cubes
½ C mayonnaise, or to taste

3 to 4 T mango chutney
¾ C golden raisins
¾ to 1 C walnuts or pecans, coarsely chopped
Salt and pepper, to taste

Place apples in a large bowl and drizzle with lemon juice. Add chicken or turkey and fold in the remaining ingredients.

Hint: *This salad makes a nice sandwich or is delicious on a bed of greens. When you are in a hurry or it is too hot to cook, buy a cooked chicken or roasted turkey breast at your local supermarket. Low fat mayonnaise tastes fine in this recipe.*

Broccoli Salad

Salad:

4 to 5 C broccoli florets
½ C celery, diced
½ C red onion, diced

½ C raisins
½ walnuts, coarsely chopped

Dressing:

1 C mayonnaise
½ C sugar

½ C vinegar

Place salad ingredients in a large bowl. Whisk dressing ingredients together and pour over the salad. Mix well. Cover and refrigerate for several hours, or if possible, for a day before serving.

Hint: *To reduce fat, use low fat mayonnaise.*

Oriental Noodle Salad

Salad:

1 lb Oriental noodles
2 to 2$\frac{1}{2}$ T sesame oil
3 to 4 scallions, thinly
 sliced on the diagonal
1 C mushrooms, thinly sliced

2 to 3 stalks celery, thinly sliced
 on the diagonal
1 red pepper, thinly sliced
1 C cooked beef, chicken or
 shrimp, sliced (optional)

Dressing:

1 to 2 tsp black pepper
1 tsp rice vinegar
 or plain white vinegar
2 T sesame paste (tahini)
 or smooth peanut butter
$\frac{1}{4}$ C warm water
$\frac{1}{2}$ C dry sherry

$\frac{1}{3}$ C soy sauce
$\frac{1}{3}$ C peanut oil or canola oil
1 heaping T fresh ginger,
 peeled and minced
1 to 2 tsp garlic, minced
2 tsp sugar

Cook noodles in boiling salted water until al dente, about 1 to 2 minutes. Drain, rinse under cool water and drain again. Toss noodles in a large bowl with sesame oil. Cover and set aside. In a medium bowl, whisk together sesame paste or peanut butter with the warm water until smooth. Stir in sherry, soy sauce, oil, ginger, garlic, sugar, vinegar and black pepper. Pour dressing over noodles. Add scallions (reserving some for garnish), celery, mushrooms and optional beef, chicken or shrimp. Toss to combine. Cover and chill for several hours, or overnight. Serve cold or at room temperature. Garnish with reserved scallions

Hint: *When Oriental noodles are not available, medium egg noodles or linguine are a good substitute. If you prefer a spicier flavor, add $\frac{1}{2}$ to 1 teaspoon dried red pepper flakes.*

Ginger Salad Dressing
or Marinade

2 scallions, chopped
2 garlic cloves, chopped
1" to $1\frac{1}{2}$" piece of ginger,
  peeled and sliced
$\frac{1}{3}$ C seasoned rice vinegar

3 T soy sauce
1 T honey
2 T sesame oil
$\frac{1}{2}$ C canola oil
Salt and pepper, to taste

Combine ingredients in a food processor and purée until well blended. Serve over any combination of salad greens. Chicken breasts can be marinated in some of this dressing, grilled, sliced and then put on top of the greens.

Hint: *This dressing tastes best if refrigerated for at least 3 hours, or up to several days, before serving.*

Sesame Salad Dressing
and Marinade

$\frac{1}{3}$ C canola or peanut oil
3 T cider vinegar
$\frac{1}{4}$ C soy sauce
2 T water
1 T sesame seeds, toasted

$1\frac{1}{2}$ tsp sesame oil
1 clove garlic, minced
1 T scallion, minced
$1\frac{1}{2}$ tsp ginger, minced

Combine all ingredients in a food processor and process until blended. Refrigerate until serving time.

Hint: *This dressing is delicious on bok choy, peapods, Chinese cabbage and bean sprouts. It can also be used to dress greens of any kind or as a marinade for swordfish, salmon or shrimp. To use as a marinade, marinate fish for about 1 hour and then broil or grill.*

Balsamic Double Vinaigrette

2 T balsamic vinegar

$\frac{1}{4}$ C red wine vinegar

$1\frac{1}{2}$ tsp Dijon mustard

$\frac{1}{2}$ C olive oil

Dash sugar

Salt and pepper, to taste

Combine all ingredients in a tightly covered jar and shake well. Refrigerate for several hours or up to a week in advance of serving.

Hint: This dressing is delicious over any salad greens, blanched drained vegetables such as green beans or asparagus or combined with cooked and drained grains and legumes such as barley, lentils, couscous or chickpeas.

Lentil Salad

$1\frac{1}{2}$ C lentils

1 medium onion, diced

$\frac{1}{3}$ to $\frac{1}{2}$ C vinaigrette salad dressing

2 T fresh parsley, chopped

2 T fresh oregano, chopped or

2 tsp dried oregano

Salt and pepper, to taste

Bring a large pot of water to a boil. Add the lentils. When the water returns to a boil, lower the heat and cook the lentils for 20 to 25 minutes, or until tender. Drain well and transfer to a serving bowl. Add onion, enough vinaigrette to moisten the mixture, parsley and oregano. Add salt and pepper, to taste. Cover and set aside for at least 30 minutes before serving or refrigerate for up to 24 hours. Before serving, taste to see if more vinaigrette is needed.

Hint: **Balsamic Double Vinaigrette** *(see above) or any vinaigrette, preferably one containing balsamic vinegar, can be used. Lentils, which are a good source of protein, are one of the few legumes that does not need to be soaked before using.*

■ ■

Barley Salad

$2\frac{1}{2}$ C chicken broth
$1\frac{1}{4}$ C barley
2 large tomatoes, chopped
$\frac{1}{4}$ C sun dried tomatoes, chopped
1 C red, yellow, orange, green or any
   combination of peppers, cubed

3 scallions, chopped
$\frac{1}{2}$ C parsley, finely minced
3 to 4 T olive oil, or to taste
$\frac{1}{4}$ C red wine vinegar
$\frac{1}{4}$ to $\frac{1}{2}$ tsp sugar
Salt and pepper, to taste

Bring broth to a boil and add the barley. Cover pot and cook over low heat for about 30 minutes, or until barley has absorbed all the broth. Cool slightly and fluff with a fork. Add remaining ingredients and toss well. Serve at room temperature.

Hint: *This salad is colorful, tasty and healthy. You can prepare this several hours ahead of serving and keep it at room temperature or make it a day ahead. Refrigerate and bring to room temperature when serving. An easy way to chop the sun dried tomatoes is to cut them with a scissors.*

Curried Tomato and Rice Salad

Salad:

2 C cooked brown or basmati rice
1 tomato, cubed

1 scallion, minced
2 to 3 T fresh parsley, minced

Place all ingredients in a medium bowl.

Dressing:

$2\frac{1}{2}$ T olive oil
3 T cider vinegar
1 tsp lemon juice

1 tsp curry powder
Salt and pepper, to taste

Whisk dressing ingredients together in a small bowl or shake in a covered jar. Pour over salad mixture and season, to taste. Refrigerate for several hours and serve on a bed of lettuce.

Black Bean and Rice Salad

$1\frac{1}{2}$ C cooked rice
2 to $2\frac{1}{4}$ C (19 oz can) black beans,
  rinsed and drained
$1\frac{1}{2}$ T olive oil
$\frac{1}{4}$ C red wine vinegar
4 scallions, chopped

1 C red, green or orange peppers or
  combination of colors, chopped
2 garlic cloves, minced
$\frac{1}{4}$ C parsley, chopped
$\frac{1}{2}$ tsp salt, or to taste
Black or white pepper, to taste

After cooking, allow rice to cool to lukewarm or use leftover cold rice. Combine remaining ingredients and add to rice. Chill for at least 1 to 2 hours before serving. Serve over lettuce.

Hint: *To make this recipe "quick and easy," chop the scallions, parsley and garlic in a food processor. For added flavor, when cooking the rice, substitute chicken broth for the water.*

Spinach Salad With Raisins and Peanuts

Featured in Cover Photo

10 oz fresh spinach
1 T vinegar
$1\frac{1}{2}$ to 2 T olive or canola oil
2 T water
1 T sugar

$\frac{1}{2}$ to 1 tsp curry powder, or to taste
1 T chutney
$\frac{1}{4}$ C raisins
$\frac{1}{4}$ C peanuts
1 apple, unpeeled, cored and diced

Wash and dry spinach and tear into bite-size pieces. Place dressing ingredients in a jar and shake well. In a large bowl, toss spinach, raisins, peanuts and apples. Add dressing and toss well.

Variations:

- Substitute 1 C sliced strawberries for the apple.
- Substitute dried cranberries for the raisins.
- Substitute chopped pecans or sliced almonds for the peanuts.

Hint: *This dressing can be made several days in advance and refrigerated.*

■ ■ ■■ ■ ■■ ■

Black Bean and Corn Salad

Featured in Cover Photo

19 oz can black beans, drained
15 oz can corn kernels, drained
2 large tomatoes, diced
2 scallions, diced
1½ tsp cumin

1½ tsp oregano
½ to 1 tsp red pepper flakes
3 to 4 T lime juice
Salt and pepper, to taste

Combine all ingredients and allow to marinate for at least a couple of hours.
Refrigerate until serving time. This keeps for at least 2 days.

Hint: *You can adjust the "heat" or spiciness of this recipe to suit your own taste by adding more cumin and red pepper flakes, if desired. Lemon juice can be substituted for the lime juice.*

Oriental Cole Slaw

Salad:

4 C green cabbage (½ medium cabbage)
  thinly sliced or shredded

2 C carrots, shredded (4 large carrots)
2 scallions, sliced

Dressing:

½ C rice vinegar
3 T sugar
1½ tsp ginger, finely minced

½ tsp salt
½ tsp red pepper flakes
2 to 3 tsp sesame oil

Place vegetables in a salad bowl. Whisk dressing ingredients together and pour over veggies. Marinate in the refrigerator for a minimum of 2 hours before serving.

■■■■■■■■■■■■■■■■■■■■■■■■■■■■■■■

Sweet Potato Salad

Salad:

6 medium sweet potatoes or yams
I small onion, diced
I stalk celery, diced

$\frac{1}{2}$ C cashews or almonds,
   toasted, for garnish

Dressing:

$\frac{1}{2}$ C parsley, minced
$\frac{1}{3}$ C olive oil
2 T lemon juice, or to taste

2 tsp soy sauce
I tsp marjoram
Salt and pepper, to taste

Scrub sweet potatoes, but do not peel. Boil in a large saucepan, partially covered, for 20 to 30 minutes, or until just tender. Drain and cool until they can be handled. Peel, cool completely and dice. Place in a large bowl and add onion and celery. In a jar, combine dressing ingredients and shake well. Pour over potato mixture and toss gently. Serve at room temperature. Sprinkle nuts over salad before serving.

Hint: *Do not overcook or potatoes will become mushy. The salad can be made early in the day.*

Red Potato Salad a la Moutard

$1\frac{1}{2}$ lbs red potatoes
2 scallions, chopped
2 T Dijon mustard
I T Pommery mustard

$\frac{1}{4}$ C olive oil
2 T red wine vinegar
3 T parsley, chopped
Salt and pepper, to taste

Scrub the potatoes and cut in half. Boil just until tender, about 15 minutes. Drain and cool well. Slice into $\frac{1}{2}$-inch pieces. In a jar, combine both mustards and oil. Add red wine vinegar, scallions and parsley and shake well. Add salt and pepper, to taste. Pour this mixture over the potatoes and toss until potatoes are coated with dressing. Serve at room temperature or chill for a few hours or up to 2 days before serving.

Hint: *This potato salad is low in fat and is very flavorful!*

Versatile Balsamic Honey Salad

Salad:

Mesclun greens or red or
  green leaf lettuce
Fresh raspberries (optional)

3 T Feta or goat cheese,
  crumbled (optional)
3 T pine nuts (optional)

Wash and thoroughly dry salad greens. Place in a large bowl. Toss with dressing and sprinkle with any or all of the optional ingredients.

Dressing:

$\frac{1}{4}$ C balsamic vinegar
$\frac{1}{4}$ C olive oil
$\frac{1}{2}$ C water
1 T honey
$1\frac{1}{2}$ tsp Dijon mustard

Salt and pepper, to taste
Pinch sugar
$\frac{1}{4}$ C fresh or frozen raspberries,
  mashed or puréed (optional)

Place all ingredients in a jar. Cover tightly and shake well. Refrigerate for several hours or up to several days. If you plan to use the raspberries, you might want to place all the ingredients in a blender or food processor so that the berries are well blended into the dressing. Transfer dressing to a jar and refrigerate.

Hint: *At first glance, it may seen that there is an error in the dressing recipe because there is very little oil and a large amount of water. This was intentionally done in order to lower the fat.*

Basil and Spinach Salad

6 C spinach leaves
$1\frac{1}{2}$ C basil leaves
$\frac{1}{4}$ C olive oil
3 cloves garlic, crushed

$\frac{1}{3}$ C pine nuts (pignoli)
Salt and pepper, to taste
$\frac{1}{3}$ to $\frac{1}{2}$ C fresh Parmesan cheese, grated

Toss the spinach and basil together in a large bowl. Heat the oil in a skillet and add garlic and pine nuts. Sauté until the nuts begin to brown slightly. Pour oil mixture over the greens and sprinkle with Parmesan cheese. Toss immediately and season to taste with salt and pepper.

■ ■

Broken Glass Jello Mold

3 oz pkg blueberry, grape or
  black raspberry Jello
3 oz pkg cherry, strawberry or
  raspberry Jello
3 oz pkg lime Jello

3 oz pkg orange, peach or apricot Jello
6 C boiling water, divided
(3) 3 oz pkgs lemon Jello
1 pt sour cream
20 oz can crushed pineapple, undrained

Individually mix the first 4 packets of Jello with $1\frac{1}{2}$ cups boiling water. Pour each one into a separate ice cube tray or other shallow pan. Chill until firm, at least 2 hours. In a very large bowl, combine 3 packages of lemon Jello with 2 cups boiling water. Stir until Jello is well dissolved. Add the sour cream and whisk until completely blended. Fold in canned pineapple with its juice. Cut each tray of firm Jello into small cubes. Remove from trays and fold into lemon Jello mixture. Ladle the mixture into a 12-cup mold or into 2 smaller molds. Chill until firm.

Hint: *You can change the flavors or colors of the Jello to suit your taste. To lower fat, use reduced fat sour cream.*

Lemon Bavarian Jello Mold

(2) 3 oz pkgs lemon Jello
6 oz can frozen lemonade concentrate
3 C boiling water

12 to 14 oz frozen whipped
  topping, defrosted

Pour Jello into a large bowl. Add boiling water and stir until completely dissolved. Add frozen lemonade and stir until melted. Refrigerate until slightly thickened, about 1 to $1\frac{1}{2}$ hours. Using an electric mixer, fold defrosted whipped topping into Jello mixture until completely blended. Pour into a greased 10- to 12-cup mold. Chill until firm. Garnish with fresh berries, grapes or orange slices.

Hint: *This comes out fine if you use "light" or "low fat" whipped topping. If you prefer to make a lime flavored mold, use lime Jello and limeade. It is often difficult to find 6 oz cans of lemonade or limeade so you may have to by a 12 oz can and use only half. Just make a pitcher of lemonade or limeade with the leftover concentrate!*

■ ■

Red, White and Blue Jello Mold

3 oz pkg blueberry or blackberry Jello
2 C boiling water, divided
16 oz can blueberry pie filling
3 oz pkg lemon Jello
1 pt sour cream

3 oz pkg strawberry Jello
16 oz pkg frozen sliced strawberries in
    juice, defrosted
Fresh strawberries, blueberries, raspberries
    or red grapes, for garnish

Dissolve blueberry or blackberry Jello in 1 cup of the boiling water. Cool slightly and fold in blueberry pie filling. Pour into a greased 10- to 12-cup Jello mold. Chill until firm. Dissolve lemon Jello in remaining cup of boiling water and cool slightly. Whisk in sour cream until completely blended. Pour over first layer of Jello. Chill until firm. Dissolve strawberry Jello in boiling water and cool slightly. Fold in defrosted berries and mix well. Pour over firm lemon Jello mixture. Chill until firm. When ready to serve, dip mold into a bath of hot water for a few seconds, or just enough to loosen Jello around the edges. Invert mold onto a serving platter. Garnish with fresh strawberries, blueberries, raspberries or red grapes, if desired.

Hint: *You can successfully substitute low fat sour cream in this recipe without sacrificing flavor. This is fun to serve on Memorial Day or The Fourth of July.*

Raspberry Cherry Jello Mold

(2) 3 oz pkgs raspberry Jello
(1) 3 oz pkg lemon Jello
1¼ C boiling water

1 pt sour cream
20 oz can pitted bing cherries
20 oz can crushed pineapple

Drain fruits well over a colander or strainer that is placed over a large bowl. Dissolve Jello in boiling water and add juices from drained fruit. Whisk in the sour cream until it is completely blended. Fold in fruit and pour into a greased 5- or 6-cup mold. Refrigerate until set. To serve, unmold onto a platter and garnish with green and purple grapes.

Hint: *You can substitute low fat sour cream for regular sour cream, but reduce the water to 1 cup.*

Apricot Dream Jello Mold

28 oz can apricot halves,
  drained (reserve juice)
(2) 3 oz pkgs apricot Jello

1 C sour cream
1 C vanilla ice cream, softened

Add enough water to reserved apricot liquid to measure 2 cups. Purée apricots in a blender or processor and set aside. Boil juice mixture. Add Jello and stir until it is completely dissolved. Cool slightly. Add sour cream and ice cream and whisk until thoroughly blended. Fold in puréed apricots. Pour into a greased 5-cup mold and refrigerate until firm. Unmold by placing in hot water for a few seconds. Invert onto a serving platter.

Hint: *This Jello mold is nice served either as part of a meal or as a dessert. Low fat sour cream can be used.*

Orange Whipped Jello

1 envelope unflavored gelatin
$\frac{1}{4}$ C sugar
Dash salt

$1\frac{3}{4}$ C hot orange juice (150°)
Whipped topping or cream,
  for garnish (optional)

In a large mixing bowl, combine gelatin, sugar and salt. Add orange juice and stir until gelatin dissolves. Chill until slightly thickened, about $1\frac{1}{2}$ hours. Using an electric mixer, beat on medium speed until mixture is light and fluffy. Ladle into dessert dishes and chill until firm. Top with a dollop of whipped topping, if desired.

Hint: *This fat free dessert is much more appealing than plain orange Jello!*

BREADS, MUFFINS AND SCONES

Portuguese Sweet Bread

2 pkg yeast
$\frac{1}{4}$ C warm (105° to 115°) water
Pinch sugar
1 C milk, scalded
1 strip lemon rind
$\frac{1}{2}$ C butter, softened and cut
  into small pieces

3 eggs
1 C sugar
6 to 6$\frac{1}{2}$ C flour
1 tsp salt
1 oz whiskey
1 egg
1 T water

In a small bowl, dissolve the yeast in the warm water. Add a pinch of sugar and set the mixture aside for 10 minutes, or until foamy. Scald the milk with the lemon rind. In a large bowl, combine the scalded milk, butter and eggs. Beat until fluffy and then cool until lukewarm. Add the yeast mixture. Add 5 cups of the flour, 1 cup at a time. Add the whisky and an additional 1 to 1$\frac{1}{2}$ cups of flour, mixing until the dough forms a ball and begins to leave the sides of the bowl. If you have a dough hook on your mixer, knead the dough for several minutes in the mixer or knead by hand on a floured surface for about 10 minutes. Place the dough in a greased bowl. Cover and let rise in a warm place for 2 hours. Punch the dough down and divide into 2 pieces. Place each ball of dough in a greased 8-inch round pan. Cover and let rise for 1$\frac{1}{2}$ hours. Mix the egg and water and brush over the dough. Bake at 350° for 25 to 30 minutes, or until the bread sounds hollow when tapped. Cool on a wire rack for a few minutes, then remove the bread from the pans and cool completely.

Yield: 2 loaves

Hint: *This is an authentic recipe from a Portuguese friend. Although it is time-consuming, it is well worth the effort! This bread freezes well.*

Cinnamon Buns

Dough:

1 pkg yeast	1 tsp salt
$\frac{1}{4}$ C warm water (105° to 115°)	6 T butter or margarine
$2\frac{1}{2}$ C flour	1 C cottage cheese
$\frac{1}{4}$ C sugar	1 egg

Dissolve yeast in water and set aside. Using the plastic blade of a food processor, mix flour and sugar for a few seconds. Add butter or margarine, cottage cheese, egg and yeast mixture. Process just until blended and dough begins to form a ball around the blade. Remove dough from processor and place on a floured surface and knead into a ball, adding a little flour to prevent sticking. Roll dough into a 10"x14" rectangle. Spread filling over surface of dough and roll up the long way, jellyroll fashion. Cut into $\frac{1}{2}$-inch slices and lay slices on their sides so that cut sides face up. Place in greased muffin tins. Cover and let rise until double, about 1 to $1\frac{1}{2}$ hours. Bake at 400° for 12 to 14 minutes, or until golden. Frost with glaze immediately. Cool in pans for about 10 minutes and transfer to a wire rack.

Filling:

3 T butter or margarine, melted	$\frac{1}{2}$ tsp almond or vanilla extract
$\frac{3}{4}$ C brown sugar	$\frac{2}{3}$ C walnuts or pecans, chopped

Melt butter or margarine and add remaining ingredients.

Glaze:

$\frac{1}{2}$ C confectioners' sugar, sifted	$\frac{1}{2}$ tsp vanilla
1 T hot water	

Blend together, adding more water if needed to make a spreadable consistency. Brush on hot buns.

Yield: 15 buns

Hint: *If you don't have a food processor, you can make the dough in a mixer or by hand.*

Challah (Jewish Egg Bread)

2 C warm water (105° to 115°)
3 pkgs yeast
8 to 10 C flour, divided
1½ C sugar, divided

1½ tsp salt
1 C butter or margarine
5 eggs, beaten (reserve 1 for glaze)

In a very large bowl, combine water and yeast and mix . Add 3 cups of flour and 1 cup of sugar. Stir well and let rise in a warm place for 30 minutes. In another bowl, combine the remaining 5 cups of flour, salt and remaining ½ cup sugar. Add the butter or margarine and cut it in with a fork or your fingers until the mixture resembles coarse meal. At the end of the half hour, add 4 of the beaten eggs to the yeast mixture. Add the flour and butter or margarine mixture to the yeast mixture. With a wooden spoon, stir the mixture together until it is no longer sticky. It may be necessary to add as much as 1 to 2 additional cups of flour. Transfer dough from the bowl to a floured surface and knead the dough until it becomes smooth and elastic. Place dough in a greased bowl and cover with a towel or plastic wrap. Let rise in a warm place for 1½ to 2 hours, or until doubled in size. Punch down. Knead for 1 to 2 minutes. Divide the dough into as many challot as you want. Braid each loaf and place in well-greased pans or on well-greased cookie sheets. Dough can be shaped into oblong or round loaves. Cover and let rise for 1 to 2 hours. Brush the tops of the challot with the remaining beaten egg and bake at 350° for 28 to 32 minutes for the medium challot or longer for the larger ones. Keep checking so that they don't burn. Loaves are done when they are tapped and sound hollow. Remove from the oven and immediately remove from pans. Cool on wire racks.

Yield: (4) 9"x5" medium loaves or 2 large loaves and 1 medium loaf
or 1 huge loaf (for a wedding or Bar/Bat Mitzvah)

Hint: *If you like, you can knead in raisins before the first rising. Also, you can freeze the challot after they are shaped, but not baked. The day you want to bake them, let them defrost and rise in a warm place until doubled in size and then glaze and bake. One way to create a warm enough place for the dough to rise is to turn on your oven to 200° for about 5 minutes and then shut it off.*

One-Bowl-and-One-Rising
Whole Wheat Bread

2 pkgs yeast
1 C warm water (105° to 115°)
1 C warm milk (105° to 115°)
3 T honey
$1\frac{1}{2}$ tsp butter or margarine
2 tsp salt

$1\frac{1}{2}$ tsp basil (optional)
3 C white flour
2 C whole wheat flour
2 tsp milk
1 tsp sesame or poppy seeds

Dissolve yeast in water and set aside. Put warm milk, honey, margarine, salt and basil in the large bowl of an electric mixer and stir until salt is dissolved and butter or margarine is melted. Cool to lukewarm. Add yeast mixture. Add half of each flour. Beat at medium speed for 2 minutes until smooth. Add remaining flour and beat until blended. Cover with a towel or plastic wrap and let rise until doubled, about 45 to 50 minutes. Preheat oven to 400°. Beat batter for 1 minute and place in a greased 9"x5" loaf pan or a 2-quart round casserole dish or stainless steel bowl. Brush top with milk and sprinkle with seeds. Reduce oven to 375° and place pan in oven. Bake for 45 to 50 minutes. Remove bread from pan immediately and cool on a wire rack.

Yield: 1 loaf

Hint: *This bread is easier and quicker to make than most yeast breads because it can be kneaded in an electric mixer and only requires 1 rising.*

Anadama Bread

$\frac{1}{2}$ C corn meal
1 C cold water, divided
1 pkg yeast
$1\frac{1}{2}$ C warm water (105° to 115°)
3 T butter or margarine

$\frac{1}{2}$ C molasses
2 tsp salt
3 C whole wheat flour
3 to $3\frac{1}{4}$ C white flour
1 to $1\frac{1}{2}$ tsp canola oil

In a small bowl, combine the corn meal and $\frac{3}{4}$ cup of the cold water. In a very small bowl or measuring cup, soften the yeast in the remaining $\frac{1}{4}$ cup of the cold water. In a saucepan, bring warm water to a boil and add the corn meal mixture. Remove from heat and add the butter or margarine, molasses and salt. Cool until lukewarm and pour into a large bowl. Add the dissolved yeast and whole wheat flour. Mix and add enough of the white flour to make a firm dough. Knead by hand on a floured board or in a mixer with a dough hook until dough is smooth. Cover with a towel or plastic wrap and let rise until doubled, about 45 minutes to 1 hour. Knead briefly and place in 2 greased loaf pans or on greased cookie sheets. Brush with oil. Cover and let rise until doubled, for about 1 hour. Bake at 400° for 15 minutes, reduce temperature to 375° and bake for about 35 additional minutes. Remove from pans immediately and cool on wire racks.

Yield: 2 loaves

Hint: *A thermometer is helpful when using yeast because the temperature of the liquid is crucial. It must be warm enough to activate the yeast, but not too hot or it will kill the yeast.*

Easy Oatmeal Bread or Rolls

$2\frac{2}{3}$ to 3 C all-purpose flour
2 pkgs yeast
2 tsp salt
$1\frac{1}{2}$ C water
$\frac{1}{3}$ C molasses
4 tsp butter or margarine

$\frac{2}{3}$ C quick rolled oats
$1\frac{1}{3}$ C whole wheat flour
1 egg, slightly beaten
1 tsp water
2 T quick rolled oats

In a large mixer bowl, combine 2 cups all-purpose flour, yeast and salt. Mix well. In a saucepan, heat $1\frac{1}{2}$ cups water, molasses and butter or margarine until very warm (115° to 120°). The butter or margarine does not need to melt. Add to flour mixture. Blend at low speed until moistened. Beat 3 minutes at medium speed. Gradually stir in whole wheat flour, oats and enough remaining all-purpose flour to make a firm dough. Continue beating with an electric mixer or knead on a floured surface for 5 to 8 minutes. Dough will be slightly sticky. Place in a greased bowl, turning to grease the top of the dough. Cover. Let rise in a warm place for about 30 minutes. Punch down dough. Divide into 2 parts. Shape each part into a round loaf or into 10 to 12 balls. Place round loaves on a greased cookie sheet or place balls of dough into a greased 8-inch round or square pan. Cover. Let rise in a warm place for about 40 minutes. Combine egg and 1 teaspoon water. Brush tops with egg mixture. Sprinkle with rolled oats. Bake at 400° for 20 to 25 minutes, or until a toothpick, inserted in the center, comes out clean. Remove from pans and cool.

Yield: 2 loaves bread or 20 to 24 rolls

Hint: *If you prefer oblong loaves of bread, you can use (2) 9"x5" loaf pans. However, these will take about 5 minutes longer to bake.*

■ ■

Speedy Soft Pretzels

I pkg dry yeast
$1\frac{1}{4}$ C warm (105° to 115°) water
I T sugar
I tsp salt

4 C flour, divided
I egg
I tsp water
Kosher or coarse salt

Place yeast in a large bowl or an electric mixer. Add water, sugar and let sit until foamy, about 10 minutes. Add flour and mix well. Place the dough on a floured surface and knead it until it is smooth and no longer sticky. Cut the dough into 16 pieces and shape as desired. Place on 2 greased or foil-lined cookie sheets. Beat the egg and water together and brush on the dough. Sprinkle with kosher or coarse salt. Bake at 425° for 13 to 16 minutes, or until golden.

Yield: 16 pretzels

Hint: *This is a quick version of pretzels and a wonderful project to do with children. The dough is fun for them to shape, plus they get to eat the pretzels soon after they've been made. They are best eaten the day they are baked. However, leftovers can be kept in a plastic bag.*

Carrot Bread

2 eggs
$\frac{3}{4}$ C sugar
$\frac{1}{2}$ C canola oil
$1\frac{1}{2}$ C flour

I tsp cinnamon
$\frac{1}{2}$ tsp salt
I tsp baking soda
$1\frac{1}{2}$ C carrots, grated (3 large carrots)

Beat eggs and sugar and mix until creamy. Add oil. Sift flour, cinnamon, salt and baking soda together and add to egg mixture. Fold in carrots. Pour dough into 3 well-greased empty 15-ounce fruit or vegetable "tin" cans, filling the cans only half way. Bake at 325° for 25 to 30 minutes, or until a toothpick, inserted in the center, comes out clean. Remove bread from the cans to a wire rack as soon as it comes out of the oven. Slice and serve with butter or cream cheese. The circular slices of bread make attractive sandwiches. This bread can also be made in (2) 3"x6" mini-loaf pans and baked for 30 to 35 minutes.

Hint: *Although this bread stays moist for several days, it is really delicious toasted. If you want to save time, you can buy shredded carrots.*

■ ■

Cranberry Orange Bread

2 C flour, sifted
1 C sugar, divided
$1\frac{1}{2}$ tsp baking powder
$\frac{1}{2}$ tsp baking soda
Dash salt
$\frac{1}{4}$ C butter or margarine, softened

$\frac{3}{4}$ C orange juice
1 T orange rind, grated (rind of 1 orange)
1 egg, well beaten
$1\frac{3}{4}$ C cranberries, chopped
$\frac{1}{2}$ C walnuts or pecans, chopped
$\frac{1}{2}$ C golden raisins (optional)

Sift flour, $\frac{3}{4}$ cups of the sugar, baking powder, baking soda and salt into a large bowl. Using a fork, cut in the butter or margarine until crumbly. In a small bowl, combine the orange juice, rind and egg. Pour into the dry ingredients and mix just until dampened. Fold in the cranberries and remaining $\frac{1}{4}$ cup sugar. Add nuts and raisins, if desired. Pour into a greased 9"x5" loaf pan and bake at 350° for 60 to 70 minutes, or until a toothpick, inserted in the center, comes out clean. If you prefer, bake in (2) 3"x6" mini-loaf pans for 45 minutes. Store overnight for easy slicing.

Hint: *You can use fresh or frozen cranberries for this recipe. However, if using frozen berries do not defrost before chopping and adding to the batter. This bread freezes well.*

Zucchini Bread

1 C canola oil
2 C sugar
3 eggs
2 C zucchini, grated
3 C flour

1 T cinnamon
1 tsp baking soda
$\frac{1}{2}$ tsp baking powder
$\frac{1}{2}$ C raisins (optional)
$\frac{1}{2}$ C walnuts, chopped (optional)

Beat oil and sugar together. Add eggs, one at a time, beating well after each addition. Add zucchini. Fold in flour, cinnamon, baking soda and baking powder. Add raisins and nuts, if desired. Pour batter into a greased 9"x5" loaf pan or (3) 3"x6" mini-loaf pans and bake at 325° for 55 to 60 minutes, or until a toothpick, inserted in the center, comes out clean.

Hint: *If using mini-pans, reduce baking time accordingly. This recipe is a wonderful way to use up surplus zucchini from your garden. This bread freezes well.*

Quick Banana Bread

2 very ripe bananas
Scant $\frac{1}{2}$ C canola oil
2 eggs
Scant 1 C sugar
$\frac{1}{4}$ C walnuts, chopped

$\frac{1}{4}$ C mini-chocolate chips
1 tsp vanilla
$1\frac{1}{4}$ C flour
1 tsp baking soda

Mash bananas in a large bowl or food processor. Add oil, eggs, sugar, nuts, chocolate chips and vanilla. Using a wooden spoon or spatula, mix well. Fold in flour and baking soda until blended. Pour into a greased 9"x5" loaf pan and bake at 350° for 45 to 55 minutes, or until a toothpick, inserted in the center, comes out clean. If you prefer, bake in (2) 3"x6" mini-loaf pans. However, reduce the baking time to 38 to 42 minutes.

Hint: *You can make this bread in only 1 bowl by using the food processor. Mash the bananas and add the remaining ingredients to the processor being careful not to overmix. If you don't have time to make this bread when your bananas are overripe, peel and freeze them for a later date. Before using, defrost and discard most of the accumulated banana juices.*

Rhubarb Nut Bread

3 eggs
1 C canola oil
$1\frac{3}{4}$ C brown sugar, firmly packed
2 tsp vanilla
$2\frac{1}{2}$ C rhubarb, finely chopped
$\frac{1}{2}$ C walnuts or pecans, chopped
2 C all-purpose flour

2 tsp baking soda
1 tsp baking powder
$\frac{1}{2}$ tsp nutmeg
1 C whole wheat flour
2 tsp cinnamon
1 tsp salt
$\frac{1}{2}$ tsp allspice

Using an electric mixer, combine eggs, oil, brown sugar and vanilla. Beat until thick and foamy. With a spoon, stir in rhubarb and nuts. In another bowl, combine remaining ingredients. Add to rhubarb mixture and stir gently just until blended. Divide the batter equally between 2 greased 9"x5" loaf pans. Bake at 350° for 40 minutes, or until a toothpick, inserted in the center, comes out clean. Cool in pans for 10 minutes. Remove from pans and cool on a wire rack.

Yield: 2 loaves

Hint: *If you prefer, use 3 cups all-purpose flour and omit the whole wheat flour.*

Corn Bread or Muffins

2 eggs
$\frac{3}{4}$ C sugar
$\frac{1}{2}$ tsp salt
$1\frac{1}{2}$ C milk
1 C corn meal

2 C flour
$4\frac{1}{2}$ tsp baking powder
$\frac{1}{2}$ C canola oil
$\frac{1}{2}$ tsp vanilla

Combine eggs, sugar, salt and milk and beat until well blended. Add corn meal, flour and baking powder, mixing just until blended. Add oil and vanilla and mix briefly. Do not overmix. Pour into a greased 9"x5" loaf pan, or a 7"x11" pan and bake at 375° for 30 minutes, or until a toothpick, inserted in the center, comes out clean. For muffins, pour batter into 18 muffin cups and bake for 18 to 20 minutes.

Hint: *You may also use (3) 3"x6" mini-loaf pans and bake for 25 minutes. Egg substitute and skim milk may be used to lower the fat in this recipe. For added flavor and texture add 1 cup fresh corn kernels.*

Morning Glory Muffins

2 C flour
$1\frac{1}{8}$ C sugar
2 tsp baking soda
2 tsp cinnamon
Dash salt
2 C carrots, grated
$\frac{1}{2}$ C raisins

$\frac{1}{2}$ C walnuts or pecans, chopped
$\frac{1}{2}$ C shredded coconut
1 apple, peeled, cored and grated
3 eggs
$\frac{3}{4}$ C canola oil
2 tsp vanilla

In a large bowl, combine flour, sugar, baking soda, cinnamon and salt. Mix in carrots, raisins, nuts, coconut and apple. In a small bowl, beat eggs, oil and vanilla. Add to dry mixture, just until the batter is combined. Do not overmix. Ladle the batter into greased muffin pans, filling to the top. Bake at 350° for 18 to 21 minutes, or until a toothpick, inserted in the center, comes out clean.

Yield: 14 muffins

Hint: *Grease the tops of the muffin pans well so that batter will not stick to the top of the pans. These muffins freeze well.*

Poppy Seed Muffins

$\frac{3}{4}$ C brown sugar

2 T butter or margarine, softened

2 eggs, lightly beaten

1 C yogurt

$\frac{3}{4}$ C raisins

$\frac{1}{2}$ C poppy seeds

1 C white flour

1 C whole wheat flour

2 tsp baking soda

$\frac{1}{2}$ tsp baking powder

In a large bowl, blend together brown sugar and butter or margarine. Add eggs, yogurt, raisins and poppy seeds and mix. Sift together flours, baking soda and baking powder and fold into poppy seed mixture until just blended. Do not overmix. Scoop batter into a greased muffin pan and bake at 400° for 15 to 17 minutes, or until a toothpick, inserted in the center, comes out clean.

Yield: 12 muffins

Hint: If you don't have whole wheat flour, you can use all white flour. Poppy seeds will keep fresh longer if they are refrigerated. Using yogurt in muffins has 2 major benefits: it helps to keep them fresh longer and often makes them lower in fat than traditional muffins.

"Big Blue" Blueberry Muffins

$\frac{1}{2}$ C butter or margarine

$\frac{1}{2}$ C sugar

2 C flour

2 eggs

$\frac{1}{2}$ C milk

1 tsp vanilla

1 T baking powder

$\frac{1}{2}$ tsp salt

$2\frac{1}{2}$ C blueberries

2 tsp sugar, for sprinkling on top

Cream butter or margarine with sugar until fluffy. Add eggs, one at a time, mixing until blended. Combine milk and vanilla. Sift dry ingredients and mix alternately with milk mixture. Mash $\frac{1}{2}$ cup of the berries and stir in by hand. Fold in remaining berries. Grease inside and tops of muffin tins. Place dough in pan and sprinkle each muffin with sugar. Bake at 375° for 30 minutes. Cool in pan for at least 30 minutes.

Yield: 12 muffins

*Hint: You can make **Apple Muffins** by substituting $2\frac{1}{2}$ cups diced apples mixed with cinnamon. To make **Cranberry Muffins**, chop 2 cups cranberries and mix with $\frac{1}{2}$ cup confectioners' sugar. Allow to sit for 30 minutes and then drain off liquid. Add to muffin mixture instead of blueberries.*

■ ■

Doughnut Muffins

$\frac{1}{3}$ C butter or margarine
1 C sugar
1 egg
1$\frac{1}{2}$ C flour, sifted

1$\frac{1}{2}$ tsp baking powder
Dash salt
$\frac{1}{4}$ tsp cinnamon or nutmeg
$\frac{1}{2}$ C milk

Topping:

6 T butter or margarine, melted
$\frac{1}{3}$ C sugar

$\frac{3}{4}$ to 1 tsp cinnamon

Cream butter or margarine with sugar. Add egg and beat until fluffy. Sift flour, baking powder, salt and cinnamon or nutmeg. Add to batter alternately with milk. Fill well-greased muffin pans two-thirds full. Bake at 400° for 17 to 19 minutes, or until golden. Remove from pan and immediately dip into melted butter or margarine and then into sugar and cinnamon, which have been combined. Serve immediately or cool on a wire rack.

Yield: 12 doughnuts

Hint: *These "doughnuts" take less time and cleanup than regular doughnuts and are much healthier. They are fun to make with children because they enjoy rolling them in the topping, as well as eating them!*

Applesauce Mini-Muffins

6 T butter or margarine
$\frac{1}{2}$ C packed brown sugar
2 eggs
$\frac{1}{2}$ C applesauce
$\frac{3}{4}$ C flour

$\frac{3}{4}$ tsp baking powder
$\frac{1}{2}$ tsp baking soda
$\frac{3}{4}$ tsp cinnamon
$\frac{1}{2}$ C raisins
$\frac{3}{4}$ C crispy rice cereal

Cream butter or margarine with sugar until fluffy. Beat in eggs and applesauce until well blended. Add remaining ingredients. Pour batter into greased mini-muffin pans and bake at 350° for 18 to 20 minutes, or until a toothpick, inserted in the center, comes out clean.

Yield: 24 mini-muffins

Hint: *These low fat muffins are very tasty and freeze well.*

Fat Free Corn Muffins

1 C corn meal	2 C flour
2 C nonfat yogurt or buttermilk	2 tsp baking powder
2 egg whites	1 tsp baking soda
$\frac{3}{4}$ C sugar	$\frac{1}{2}$ tsp salt

In a large bowl, combine corn meal and yogurt or buttermilk. In another bowl, beat egg whites until foamy. Add sugar and beat for another minute. Stir in corn meal mixture. Add flour, baking powder and baking soda and mix just until blended. Do not overmix or muffins will be tough. Spoon the batter into greased muffin pans. Bake at 400° for 20 to 25 minutes, or until golden and center of muffins springs back when touched. Cool pan on a wire rack for 10 to 15 minutes. Remove muffins from pan and allow to cool completely.

Yield: 15 muffins

Healthy Scones

1 C flour	Dash salt
$\frac{1}{2}$ C oatmeal	2 T margarine
$\frac{1}{2}$ C corn meal	$\frac{1}{3}$ C raisins, dried cranberries or
3 T sugar, divided	dried cherries
1 tsp baking powder	1 egg
$\frac{1}{2}$ tsp baking soda	$\frac{2}{3}$ C yogurt or buttermilk

In a large bowl, combine flour, oatmeal, corn meal, 2 tablespoons of the sugar, baking powder, baking soda and salt. With a pastry blender or fork, cut in margarine until mixture resembles coarse meal. Add raisins, dried cranberries or dried cherries. In a small bowl, whisk egg and yogurt or buttermilk together. Add to flour mixture and stir just until dry mixture is moistened. Drop by $\frac{1}{4}$-cup amounts onto a greased cookie sheet. Sprinkle with remaining tablespoon of sugar. Bake at 350° for 18 to 20 minutes, or until lightly golden at the edges. Serve warm or reheat just before serving. Serve with raspberry jam or jams or jellies of your choice.

Yield: 10 scones

Hint: *If you use an egg substitute and nonfat yogurt, these scones will be very low in fat.*

Scones

1$\frac{3}{4}$ C flour
2$\frac{1}{2}$ tsp baking powder
1$\frac{1}{2}$ T sugar
$\frac{1}{2}$ tsp salt

6 T butter or margarine, softened
2 eggs
$\frac{1}{3}$ C light cream
$\frac{3}{4}$ C raisins

Sift flour and mix with baking powder, sugar and salt. Cut in the butter or margarine with a fork. In a separate bowl, beat eggs. Add eggs and cream to dry ingredients and mix until combined. Add raisins and knead briefly with your hands. On a floured surface, pat dough (with floured hands) to $\frac{3}{4}$-inch thickness. Using a 2- to 3-inch biscuit or cookie cutter, cut dough into 10 or 11 scones. Place on an ungreased cookie sheet. Bake at 425° for 10 to 12 minutes, or until golden. Serve hot with sweet butter or jam.

Yield: 10 or 11 scones

Hint: *This is one recipe where butter is really preferable to margarine, both in terms of taste and texture.*

Date Scones

2 C flour
1 T sugar
2$\frac{1}{2}$ tsp baking powder
Dash salt

3 T butter or margarine, divided
$\frac{2}{3}$ C milk
1 C dates, chopped

Sift dry ingredients into a bowl. With a fork or your fingertips, blend in 2 tablespoons of the butter or margarine. Add milk, stirring with a fork. Knead slightly to make a soft dough. Roll out half of the dough $\frac{1}{2}$ inch thick. Spread with dates. Roll out other half of dough to same thickness and place on top of the dates. Roll up dough jellyroll fashion and roll out into a square. Cut into 4 smaller squares and cut each square on the diagonal so that each scone is triangular in shape. Melt remaining tablespoon of butter or margarine and brush on the tops of the scones. Place on a greased cookie sheet and bake at 450° for 10 minutes, or until golden in color. Serve with butter or jam

Yield: 8 scones

Hint: *These are much easier to make than they sound. They only take about 10 minutes to prepare. Dried cranberries or currants may be substituted for the dates.*

■■■■■■■■■■■■■■■■■■■■■■■■■■■■■■■

EGGS AND CHEESE

Stuffed French Toast

1 loaf challah * (not braided), sliced

Filling:

8 oz cream cheese
2 T sugar

$\frac{1}{2}$ C walnuts, chopped (optional)
1 tsp vanilla

Coating:

$1\frac{1}{2}$ C milk or all-purpose cream
6 eggs
$\frac{1}{4}$ to $\frac{1}{2}$ tsp nutmeg

Few T butter or margarine,
for frying French toast

Sauce:

12 oz apricot jam

$\frac{1}{2}$ C orange juice

Beat cream cheese, sugar and vanilla until fluffy. Add walnuts, if desired. Cut challah slices into quarters. Spread filling on half of the challah pieces. Top with remaining pieces. Beat coating mixture together. Using tongs, dip "challah sandwiches" into coating and then fry in hot butter or margarine until golden. Turn and fry on the other side until golden. Make sauce by combining apricot jam and orange juice in a microwaveable bowl and cooking on high, or by cooking on top of the stove, stirring occasionally, until blended. Serve French toast with warm sauce.

Yield: Approx. 40 French toast quarters

* Challah is traditional Jewish bread. See recipe pg. 53.

Hint: *To reduce fat and cholesterol you can use light cream cheese, egg substitute, low fat milk and omit the walnuts. To prepare in advance, cool the French toast and then freeze in a foil pan. To serve, spread frozen French toast quarters on a cookie sheet and heat at 350° until hot.*

Egg Foo Yong

Pancakes:

5 eggs, unbeaten
$\frac{1}{2}$ C cooked beef, chicken, pork, shrimp,
   thinly sliced (optional)
$\frac{1}{2}$ C celery ($\frac{1}{2}$ stalk), shredded or
   thinly sliced
1 C bean sprouts

$\frac{1}{2}$ C mushrooms, shredded
   or thinly sliced
1 small onion, shredded or finely chopped
1 tsp dry sherry
Salt and pepper, to taste
$\frac{1}{2}$ to 1 C canola or peanut oil

Combine all ingredients, except oil, in a large bowl. Mix gently. Heat oil in a wok or fry pan until hot. Place about one-quarter of egg mixture into hot oil and fry until golden on 1 side. Turn over and fry other side until golden. Drain on paper towels. Serve with sauce. Alternately, make one "family style" pancake by cooking entire mixture at once.

Sauce:

14 oz chicken or vegetable broth
1 tsp ketchup
1 T soy sauce

$\frac{1}{4}$ tsp salt (optional)
$2\frac{1}{2}$ T flour
$\frac{1}{4}$ C cold water

Place all ingredients except flour and cold water in a saucepan. Whisk together flour and water and add to pan. Cook over medium heat, stirring constantly, until mixture begins to boil and thicken.

Microwave Instructions: Place all ingredients in a microwaveable bowl or large measuring cup and cook on high, stirring occasionally, for about 2 minutes, or until thick and bubbly.

Hint: You can make the pancake "heart healthy" by using an egg substitute, reducing oil to 1 to 2 tablespoons and by using low sodium soy sauce. To make the sauce healthier, use low sodium broth, low sodium ketchup and low sodium soy sauce.

■■■■■■■■■■■■■■■■■■■■■■■■■■■■■■■

Baked Cheese Blintz

Base:

$\frac{1}{2}$ C butter or margarine, melted
$\frac{1}{2}$ C sugar
6 eggs
1 C flour

$\frac{1}{4}$ C milk
1 T baking powder
$\frac{1}{2}$ tsp vanilla
Dash salt

Topping:

6 oz part skim ricotta cheese
4 oz cream cheese, softened
2 T lemon juice ($\frac{1}{2}$ lemon)

1 tsp lemon rind, grated (1 lemon)
$\frac{1}{4}$ C sugar
2 eggs

In a large microwaveable bowl, melt butter or margarine. Remove from microwave. Whisk in sugar, eggs, flour, milk, baking powder, vanilla and salt until well blended. Pour into a greased 9"x13" baking pan. In a food processor or blender, beat ricotta cheese, cream cheese, lemon juice, lemon rind, sugar and eggs until smooth. Pour cheese mixture over mixture in baking pan, spreading carefully to cover. Bake at 300° for 50 to 60 minutes, or until set. Cool slightly before cutting. If desired, top with berries.

Hint: *To make a smaller blintz, cut the recipe in half and bake in an 8-inch square pan. Reduce baking time to about 45 minutes. Light cream cheese may be used in this recipe. Also, leftovers may be reheated at 350° for about 10 minutes, or until hot.*

Dried Berry Waffles

$1\frac{3}{4}$ C flour
1 T baking powder
$\frac{1}{4}$ tsp salt (optional)
2 eggs

$1\frac{1}{4}$ C milk
3 to 4 T canola oil
1 C dried berries (cranberries,
   cherries or blueberries)

Combine dry ingredients and set aside. Using a whisk or electric mixer, beat eggs, milk and oil until light. Pour into dry mixture and mix just until blended. Fold in dried berries. Pour onto a greased waffle iron and cook according to manufacturer's directions.

Yield: 3 large waffles

Hint: *Leftover waffles may be frozen.*

Artichoke Frittata

(2) 6 oz jars marinated artichokes,
   drained and chopped
1 small onion, chopped
2 cloves garlic, minced
4 eggs
Dash Tabasco

Salt and pepper, to taste
$\frac{1}{3}$ C flavored bread crumbs
1 tsp lemon juice
$\frac{1}{2}$ tsp oregano
2 T parsley, chopped
2 C Cheddar cheese, grated

Drain artichokes, reserving 2 tablespoons of the marinade. Pour marinade into a large fry pan and sauté onion and garlic until soft, not brown. Beat eggs and add remaining ingredients, including sautéed onion and garlic. Pour into a greased 9-inch pie plate or square baking dish and bake at 325° for 30 minutes, or until golden. Let stand 5 minutes before cutting.

Hint: *If you make this in a square pan, it can be cut into large squares and served for brunch or lunch or you can cut it into 1-inch squares and serve as an hors d'oeuvre. Also, you can use egg substitute for the eggs with excellent results.*

Crustless Vegetable Quiche
Featured in Cover Photo

1 T olive oil
1 eggplant, peeled and cubed
1 medium zucchini, cubed
1 large onion, diced
3 to 4 tomatoes, peeled and cubed
Salt and pepper, to taste

3 eggs
$\frac{1}{4}$ C Parmesan cheese
1 tsp oregano
1 tsp basil
1 C Mozzarella cheese, shredded

Heat oil in a large fry pan and add eggplant, zucchini and onion. Sauté for 10 minutes. Add tomatoes, cover pan and simmer for 35 or 40 minutes, or until fairly thick. Cool slightly and add salt and pepper, to taste. Combine eggs, Parmesan cheese, oregano and basil. Grease or spray a 9-inch pie plate and layer half the veggies and then half the egg mixture and repeat layers. Top with Mozzarella and bake at 350° for 40 minutes, or until firm. Let stand for 5 minutes before slicing.

Hint: *You can use egg substitute and low fat Mozzarella successfully in this recipe.*

Chili Cheese Squares

$\frac{1}{2}$ C butter or margarine
10 eggs
$\frac{1}{2}$ C flour
1 tsp baking powder

8 oz can green chilies, chopped
1 lb cottage cheese
1 lb Monterey Jack cheese, shredded

In the oven or in a microwave, melt butter or margarine in a 9"x13" pan. Beat eggs lightly in a large bowl. Whisk in flour and baking powder. Add the melted butter or margarine, chilies, cottage and Monterey Jack cheeses. Mix until blended. Pour batter into the hot pan and bake at 400° for 15 minutes. Reduce heat to 350° and bake for an additional 35 to 40 minutes, or until puffy and golden. Let sit for about 5 minutes and cut into squares. Serve hot. These may be prepared in advance, and popped into the oven when guests arrive, or baked completely in advance, cut and reheated.

Yield: 24 cheese squares

Hint: *This recipe can also be made into (2) 9-inch pies or squares, which can be cut into wedges or cut into small squares and used as hors d'oeuvres. These can be frozen. To heat, bake at 350° for 15 minutes, or until hot. Use either mild or hot chilies, depending on your taste buds.*

Cranberry Pancakes

$1\frac{1}{2}$ C flour
1 tsp salt
$\frac{1}{2}$ C sugar
$2\frac{1}{2}$ tsp baking powder
2 eggs

3 T butter or margarine, melted
1 C milk
1 C cranberries, coarsely chopped
Few T canola oil

Sift dry ingredients together. Add eggs, melted butter or margarine and milk. Stir quickly until just blended. Add cranberries. Heat oil in a fry pan and drop batter by tablespoons into the pan. Cook until tiny bubbles appear. Turn over and cook until golden.

Hint: *This batter can be made the night before. However, don't add cranberries until the morning. You can make* **Cranapple Pancakes** *by mixing $\frac{1}{2}$ cup chopped cranberries and $\frac{1}{2}$ cup diced apples.*

■ ■

Cheese and Veggie Strata

I red, green or orange pepper, diced	2 C Cheddar, Swiss, Fontina or
I medium onion, diced	Monterey Jack cheese, grated
I C mushrooms, diced	3 C milk
Few T soft butter or margarine, divided	I tsp dry mustard
12 slices bread, divided	$1\frac{1}{2}$ T Dijon mustard
5 eggs	Salt and pepper, to taste

Sauté pepper, onion and mushrooms in I tablespoon butter or margarine until softened, but not brown. Spread remaining butter or margarine on bread. Place 6 slices bread, buttered side down, in a greased 9"x13" pan. Place cheese on top of bread. Spread sautéed veggies over cheese. Place remaining 6 slices of bread, buttered side up, over veggies. Beat eggs, milk, both mustards, salt and pepper together and pour on top. Bake at 350° for 45 to 55 minutes, or until puffy and golden. Let sit for 8 to 10 minutes before cutting into squares.

Hint: To make this in advance, you can prepare it completely, cover with foil and refrigerate for several hours or overnight. Remove it from the refrigerator and then bake it as above. Also, egg substitute can be used with tasty results.

Tuna Puff

10 slices white bread	$\frac{3}{4}$ tsp dry mustard
6 eggs	Dash salt
3 C milk	(2) $6\frac{1}{2}$ oz cans tuna, packed in water
I T parsley, minced	2 C sharp Cheddar cheese, shredded

Remove crusts from bread and cut bread into cubes. Set aside. In a large bowl, whisk together eggs, milk and seasonings. Flake tuna with a fork. Add tuna, cheese and bread to egg mixture. Pour into a greased 9"x13" pan or large soufflé dish and bake at 350° for I hour, or until puffed and golden. Let sit for 8 to 10 minutes before cutting into squares.

Hint: You can cut this recipe in thirds or in half and bake it in a 9-inch pie plate or square pan. It still takes about an hour to bake. You can substitute $1\frac{1}{2}$ to 2 cups cooked, diced shrimp for the tuna.

Apple Noodle Kugel

16 oz wide noodles
6 eggs, well beaten
12 T butter or margarine,
  melted, divided
$1\frac{1}{2}$ C applesauce

6 apples, peeled and diced
$\frac{3}{4}$ C sugar
2 tsp vanilla
1 C golden raisins
Salt and pepper, to taste

Boil noodles in a large pot and drain well. Place noodles and all remaining ingredients, except 4 tablespoons of the melted butter or margarine, into the empty pot in which the noodles were cooked. Stir until everything is well combined. Pour into a greased 9"x13" pan. Drizzle remaining 4 tablespoons butter or margarine over the top of the noodle mixture. Bake at 350° for 1 hour.

Light Noodle Kugel

1 lb fine noodles
1 qt buttermilk
3 eggs
1 tsp vanilla

$\frac{1}{4}$ C sugar
Pinch salt
$\frac{1}{4}$ C butter or margarine, melted
1 C golden raisins

Boil noodles and drain. Combine remaining ingredients and fold into cooked noodles. Pour into a greased 9"x13" pan and bake at 350° for 25 minutes.

Topping:

2 C corn flakes
$\frac{1}{2}$ C butter or margarine

$\frac{1}{2}$ C brown sugar
1 tsp cinnamon

Break corn flakes with your hands and sprinkle over kugel. Heat butter or margarine, brown sugar and cinnamon in saucepan until melted. Pour the hot topping over partially cooked kugel. Put kugel back in the oven and bake for 25 additional minutes, or until golden.

Hint: *This kugel, made with buttermilk instead of cottage cheese, cream cheese and/or sour cream, is much lower in fat than most kugels, making it is also light and delicious!*

Cidered Baked French Toast

4 slices cinnamon-raisin bread
2 eggs
$\frac{1}{2}$ C apple cider or apple juice

2 T sugar
$\frac{1}{2}$ tsp vanilla
Confectioners' sugar, for sprinkling on top

Place bread in a 9-inch square baking pan. Whisk together eggs, cider, sugar and vanilla until well blended. Pour this mixture over the bread. Let stand, turning once, until egg mixture is absorbed, about 5 to 10 minutes. Place bread slices on a cookie sheet that has been greased or sprayed with a nonstick cooking spray. Bake at 375° for 12 minutes and turn slices. Continue baking until puffed and golden, approximately 12 additional minutes. Serve with applesauce or with confectioners' sugar sprinkled on top.

Hint: *If you don't have raisin bread, use plain bread and add 2 tablespoons raisins to the egg mixture. This recipe is lower in fat than traditional French toast because it is baked rather than fried. Also, egg substitutes can be used. People who are lactose intolerant will appreciate the fact that this is made with cider instead of milk.*

Cheese Fondue

1 lb Emmenthaler or Gruyere
  cheese, shredded
1 heaping T flour
1 clove garlic

$1\frac{1}{2}$ C dry white wine (Chablis, Riesling)
1 T lemon juice
Pepper and nutmeg, to taste
2 loaves French or Italian bread, cubed

Dredge cheese with flour. Rub fondue pot with cut garlic clove. Place the pot over the heating element. Pour wine into the pot and heat until the wine is hot, but not boiling. Add lemon juice. Add cheese by the handful, stirring constantly with a wooden spoon until cheese is melted and mixture is creamy. Add pepper and nutmeg, to taste. Spear fork through bread cubes and dunk into fondue pot.

Yield: 4 servings as a main course or 12 to 18 servings as a snack

Hint: *A combination of Emmenthaler and Gruyere cheese may be used.*

■ ● ■ ● ■ ● ■ ● ■ ● ■ ● ■ ● ● ■ ■ ● ■ ● ● ■ ● ● ■ ● ● ■ ■ ■ ● ● ● ● ■ ● ■ ● ■ ● ● ■ ● ■ ● ■ ■

FISH AND SEAFOOD

Poached Salmon

2 qts water
$\frac{1}{2}$ bay leaf
$\frac{1}{2}$ C celery, chopped
$\frac{1}{2}$ C vinegar or 1 C dry white wine
$\frac{1}{4}$ C carrots, chopped

1 small onion, chopped
1 tsp salt
Few sprigs parsley
3 to 4 lb salmon, tail end

In a fish poacher or large pan, bring water to a boil. Add all ingredients except the salmon. Cover and boil for 15 minutes. If not using a fish poacher, tie salmon in cheese cloth and lower gently into boiling liquid. Bring to a boil and simmer, covered, for 8 to 10 minutes per pound. Carefully remove salmon from broth. While still warm, remove skin and gray matter until pink flesh is exposed. Place on a serving platter and chill. Serve with **Versatile Dill Sauce**.

Versatile Dill Sauce

5 T mayonnaise
$\frac{1}{2}$ C yogurt
2 T vinegar

4 tsp Dijon mustard
$\frac{1}{2}$ to 1 tsp dill, finely minced

Combine all ingredients and whisk until smooth. Serve this sauce with poached salmon or any other cold fish or seafood.

Hint: *This sauce is also delicious on cooked asparagus.*

Potato-Crusted Fish

I tsp oil or nonstick cooking spray
I lb salmon, scrod or haddock fillets
I lb mashed potatoes
3 scallions, finely chopped

2 to 3 garlic cloves, finely chopped
Salt and pepper, to taste
I to 2 T Parmesan cheese, grated

Make or purchase mashed potatoes. If potatoes are cold, warm them slightly and fold in scallions, garlic, salt and pepper. Grease or spray a baking pan. Place fish in the pan, skin-side down. Spread the potato mixture over the entire surface of the fish. Sprinkle with Parmesan cheese. Place in a preheated 450° oven and bake for approximately 15 to 18 minutes, or until fish flakes. Broil just until potatoes are golden.

Hint: *This dish looks very fancy and gets rave reviews when people see it and taste it. However, it is very simple to prepare.*

Salmon With Tarragon and Tomatoes

I T olive oil
I lb salmon fillet
I small onion, chopped
2 cloves garlic, finely chopped
I tsp tarragon

3 T white wine
$\frac{1}{3}$ to $\frac{1}{2}$ C cream
2 medium tomatoes, skinned
  and chopped
Salt and pepper, to taste

Heat oil in a sauté pan until hot. Place salmon in the pan, skin-side up, and cook for 3 to 4 minutes. Turn salmon over and cook for an additional 3 to 4 minutes. Remove from the pan. Using a metal spatula, remove any skin that may have stuck to the pan. Put the pan back on the stove and add the onion and garlic and sauté until tender. Add wine and tarragon and cook for I minute. Add cream and tomatoes and place salmon back in pan. Cook for about 5 minutes, or until salmon reaches desired doneness.

Hint: *You can use light cream without sacrificing flavor. Also, you can use canned tomatoes instead of fresh ones.*

■ ■

Microwave Salmon Teriyaki

$\frac{3}{4}$ to I lb salmon fillet
2 T orange juice
2 cloves garlic, minced
I tsp fresh ginger, minced

2 T soy sauce
2 scallions, thinly sliced
2 T sesame seeds, toasted

Place salmon, skin-side down, in a microwave pan. Combine orange juice, garlic, ginger and soy sauce and pour over fish. Cover pan with plastic wrap in which you have cut 2 small holes to act as vents. Microwave on high for 7 minutes, turning once if your microwave doesn't have a carousel. Fish is done when it flakes and is no longer translucent in the middle. Cook longer, if needed. To serve, place fish on a platter and sprinkle with scallions and sesame seeds.

Hint: Low sodium soy sauce can be used in this recipe.

Greek-Style Fish

I lb scrod, haddock or other white fish
2 to 3 tsp olive oil
2 onions, sliced
3 cloves garlic, minced
2 medium tomatoes, chopped

$\frac{1}{2}$ to I tsp oregano
$\frac{1}{2}$ to $\frac{3}{4}$ C dry white wine
Salt and pepper, to taste
$\frac{1}{2}$ lemon, thinly sliced

Heat olive oil in a skillet and add onions and garlic. Sauté until translucent. Add tomatoes, oregano and wine and sauté until tomatoes are soft. Place half of this mixture in a greased 9-inch ovenproof dish. Place fish on top. Place remaining mixture on fish. Top with lemon slices. Bake at 450° for 10 minutes, or until fish is completely cooked and flakes.

Hint: To reduce the fat, use nonstick cooking spray instead of olive oil to sauté onions and garlic.

Salmon Loaf Elegante

4 slices white bread or
  challah, with crusts
1 C warm milk
5 eggs, separated
$\frac{1}{4}$ lb butter or margarine
2 large onions, chopped
10 mushrooms, sliced or
  2 oz canned, drained

14 to 15 oz can red salmon, drained
  shed and liquid reserved
2 carrots, grated
2 stalks celery, grated or chopped
1 C sour cream
8 oz canned peas, drained or frozen peas
  cooked and drained
$\frac{1}{2}$ C corn flake crumbs

Break bread into small pieces and pour milk over it. Set aside. Beat egg whites until stiff and set aside. Melt butter or margarine in a large skillet and sauté onions and mushrooms until soft, but not brown. In a medium mixing bowl, beat egg yolks, salmon, onion and mushroom mixture, carrots, celery, sour cream and peas. Add soaked bread and mix well. Add 1 tablespoon of the reserved salmon liquid. Fold in beaten egg whites. Pour into a greased 9"x13" pan and sprinkle with corn flake crumbs. Bake at 350° for 55 to 60 minutes, or until crumbs are golden and mixture is set. Cool for at least 5 minutes before cutting into squares.

Hint: *You can bake this a day in advance and reheat at 350° for 20 to 30 minutes, or until hot. Do not freeze or it will become soggy. However, if you want to make this several hours or even a day or two in advance and bake it just before serving, set the egg whites aside and prepare the rest of the recipe. If making it early in the day, keep egg whites at room temperature and beat just before adding to mixture and baking. If doing it a day or two ahead, keep egg whites covered in the refrigerator and then allow them to come to room temperature before beating and folding into salmon mixture.*

Oriental Fish Steaks

$1\frac{1}{2}$ lbs swordfish, tuna, shark or
  salmon steaks
3 T lime juice
2 T soy sauce

2 cloves garlic, minced
1 tsp fresh ginger, minced
1 tsp sesame oil
Dash chili powder

Place fish in a shallow pan. Combine all the other ingredients and pour over fish. Turn fish so that both sides are coated. Marinate in the refrigerator for 1 to 2 hours, turning a few times. Grill or broil for 5 to 6 minutes per side, or until desired doneness is reached.

■ ■

Marinated Fish Steaks With Curry

1 to 1½ lbs swordfish, halibut or
  salmon steaks
¼ tsp salt
1 tsp curry powder

1½ T olive oil
1½ tsp lemon juice
1½ tsp cider vinegar

Combine all ingredients, except fish, in a shallow pan. Place fish in pan. Turn fish over so that all sides are well coated. Marinate for 5 to 6 hours, turning occasionally. Broil or grill for 5 to 6 minutes per side, or until desired doneness is reached.

Swordfish Amandine

1 lb swordfish steaks
1 to 2 T butter or margarine
1 T lemon juice
Rind of ½ lemon, grated

1½ tsp dry sherry
1 T parsley, chopped
Dash paprika
2 T slivered almonds, toasted

Place swordfish on a greased broiling pan or grill. In a small pan, melt the butter or margarine. Add lemon juice, rind, sherry and parsley. Pour half of this mixture over the fish. Broil or grill for 7 to 8 minutes. Turn fish over and spoon on remaining sauce. Sprinkle with paprika. Broil or grill for 7 to 8 minutes, or until fish reaches desired doneness. Sprinkle with almonds.

Quick and Easy Broiled
or Grilled Fish Steaks

Spread a thin coating of mayonnaise on swordfish, tuna, halibut or salmon. Broil or grill for 5 to 6 minutes. Turn over and spread with mayonnaise. Broil or grill for an additional 5 to 6 minutes, or until fish is cooked to desired doneness.

Hint:. *For added flavor, mix mayonnaise with Dijon mustard, honeycup mustard, minced dill or freshly grated Parmesan cheese. Low fat mayonnaise works well in this recipe.*

Portuguese Fish Stew

3 onions, sliced
2 cloves garlic, minced
1 green pepper, sliced
$\frac{1}{4}$ to $\frac{1}{3}$ C olive oil
28 oz can whole tomatoes
8 oz tomato sauce
1 C water

1 C dry white wine
$1\frac{1}{2}$ to 2 lbs white fish, cut into chunks
4 T fresh parsley, or to taste
$\frac{1}{4}$ to $\frac{1}{2}$ tsp dried crushed red pepper,
  or to taste
Salt and pepper, to taste

Sauté onions, garlic and pepper in oil until soft. Mash tomatoes with a potato masher. Add to onions and pepper. Add tomato sauce, water and wine. Cook, covered, for 30 minutes. Add fish and cook for an additional 10 to 15 minutes, or until fish is tender. Add parsley during the last few minutes. Season to taste.

Hint: *Serve with crusty bread. This makes a delicious meal that is low in fat. You can use "fish pieces" or chowder fish for an economical meal.*

Tuna Risotto With Mushrooms

1 to 2 tsp olive oil
1 C mushrooms, sliced
$\frac{1}{2}$ C onion, diced
2 carrots, diced
2 cloves garlic, minced
$\frac{3}{4}$ C arborio rice
1 C clam juice, divided

$1\frac{1}{2}$ C water, divided
(2) $6\frac{1}{2}$ oz cans white tuna
  in water, drained
1 C frozen peas, defrosted
$\frac{1}{4}$ C Parmesan cheese, shredded
2 T parsley, minced
Salt and pepper, to taste

Heat olive oil in a heavy saucepan. Sauté mushrooms, onion, carrots and garlic until slightly tender. Add rice and sauté until lightly browned. Add $\frac{1}{2}$ cup of the clam juice and $\frac{1}{2}$ cup of the water. Stir often, simmering for 5 to 6 minutes, or until liquid is absorbed. Repeat this process by adding $\frac{1}{2}$ cup clam juice and $\frac{1}{2}$ cup water. Then add the last $\frac{1}{2}$ cup of water, along with tuna, peas, cheese and parsley. Stir and simmer for 3 to 5 minutes, or until liquid is absorbed. Season with salt and pepper.

Hint: *This is a healthy and modern-day version of the classic tuna casserole, however, it uses arborio rice, a short-grained rice from Italy. You can substitute 2 cups cooked, cubed chicken for the tuna.*

■ ■

Grilled Halibut Packet

1 lb halibut steak or fillets
$\frac{1}{4}$ lb mushrooms, sliced
1 T fresh ginger, minced or
  1 tsp dried ginger

2 scallions, cut into 2" pieces
$\frac{1}{2}$ small red pepper, thinly sliced
$\frac{1}{2}$ tsp sesame oil

Spray a large piece of heavy duty foil with nonstick spray. Place halibut on foil. Top with remaining ingredients. Bring 2 opposite ends of foil together and fold over tightly. Then seal the other ends. Place the packet on the hot grill and cook for 8 to 10 minutes per inch of thickness of fish, turning the packet over halfway during cooking time.

Hint: You can substitute other fish for the halibut. Also, you can cut the fish into serving-size portions and make individual packets.

Easy Broiled Fish

1 lb scrod, haddock or halibut
2 T sour cream

$\frac{1}{4}$ tsp paprika, or to taste

Place fish on a broiler pan. Spread sour cream over it. Sprinkle with paprika. Broil for 10 to 15 minutes, watching carefully so that fish doesn't burn.

Hint: Reduced fat sour cream may be substituted for regular sour cream.

Nutty Crusted Fish

$1\frac{1}{2}$ lbs halibut, swordfish, cod,
  salmon fillets or steaks
$1\frac{1}{2}$ T Dijon mustard
1 to 2 tsp butter or margarine, melted
1 T honey

$\frac{1}{4}$ C pecans or walnuts, finely chopped
3 T bread crumbs
2 tsp parsley, chopped
Salt and pepper, to taste
Lemon wedges, for garnish

In a small bowl, whisk together mustard, butter or margarine and honey. In another small bowl, combine nuts, bread crumbs and parsley. Place fish on a greased baking sheet. Brush honey mustard mixture over fish. Sprinkle with crumb mixture. Bake at 450° for 10 minutes per inch of thickness, or until fish flakes. Season with salt and pepper, to taste. Garnish with lemon wedges.

Chinese Shrimp With Mock Lobster Sauce

I lb lean ground beef	I T soy sauce
I egg	2 tsp Gravy Master
I to 1½ tsp garlic powder	¼ C water
I T sugar	⅓ lb shrimp, peeled and cooked
I C boiling beef broth	2 scallions, chopped, for garnish
2 T cornstarch	

Brown beef in a fry pan until no longer pink. Beat egg and stir into beef. Combine garlic powder, sugar and broth. Add to meat mixture in pan. In a small bowl, combine cornstarch, soy sauce, Gravy Master and water and whisk together to form gravy. Add mixture to the fry pan and mix until meat mixture is thick and fairly smooth. Lower heat to a simmer and cook, uncovered for 7 to 8 minutes. Add shrimp and cook for an additional 2 minutes, or just until shrimp are hot. Do not overcook or shrimp will get tough. Garnish with scallions. Serve over rice.

Hint: *Defrost shrimp before adding them to the sauce. The shrimp may be omitted.*

Shrimp Scampi

I lb shrimp	½ tsp oregano
2 to 3 T butter	2 T lemon juice
2 T olive oil	Salt and pepper, to taste
4 to 5 cloves garlic, minced	¼ C parsley, minced
⅓ C dry sherry	

Peel, clean and devein shrimp. Boil shrimp until tender and opaque, watching carefully to prevent overcooking. Melt butter in a large fry pan. Add olive oil, garlic and sherry and sauté until garlic is tender. Add oregano, lemon juice, salt, pepper and parsley. Add shrimp and stir just until shrimp are hot and coated with sauce. Serve over pasta.

Hint: *Traditional shrimp scampi recipes use much more butter and oil than this recipe so this recipe is lower in fat. To save time, use peeled shrimp or use cooked shrimp which should be added at the very end and heated very briefly.*

■ ■

Shrimp, Rice and Asparagus Casserole

1 C long grain rice
2 C water or chicken or vegetable broth
$\frac{3}{4}$ lb asparagus, cut into 1" pieces
$\frac{1}{2}$ lb small or medium cooked shrimp
$\frac{1}{4}$ lb mushrooms, sliced

$\frac{1}{2}$ C Romano or Parmesan cheese, grated
2 to 3 T olive oil
Salt and pepper, to taste
Paprika

In a medium saucepan, bring water or broth to a boil. Add rice, reduce heat to low and cover. Cook rice for 10 minutes. Add asparagus and cook for an additional 5 minutes. Add shrimp, mushrooms, cheese, oil, salt and pepper and fold into rice mixture. Pour into a greased 2-quart casserole. Sprinkle with paprika and bake at 450° for 12 minutes, or until hot.

Hint: For extra flavor, add more cheese and olive oil.

Shrimp Florentine

(2) 10 oz pkgs frozen chopped spinach
1 lb shrimp, cooked, shelled
  and deveined
$\frac{1}{4}$ C butter or margarine
$\frac{1}{4}$ C scallions, chopped
$\frac{1}{4}$ C flour

$1\frac{1}{2}$ C milk
$\frac{1}{2}$ C dry white wine or fish broth
1 C Swiss or Cheddar cheese, shredded
Salt and pepper, to taste
Paprika

Thaw spinach and squeeze dry. Spread spinach in a greased 9"x13" baking dish. Top with shrimp. In a medium saucepan, melt the butter or margarine, add the scallions and sauté for 1 minute. Add the flour and whisk well. Gradually add the milk and wine or broth. Cook, stirring constantly, over low heat until sauce bubbles and thickens. Add cheese and cook just until cheese melts. Season with salt and pepper. Pour sauce over the shrimp. Sprinkle with paprika. Bake at 350° for 25 to 30 minutes, or until bubbly. Let sit for a few minutes before serving.

Hint: You can make the cheese sauce in the microwave by placing the butter or margarine in a medium bowl and cooking on high for about 45 seconds, or until it melts. Cook scallions for about 10 seconds. Blend in flour and stir in milk and wine. Microwave on high for 3 to 4 minutes, or until sauce is thickened, stirring after each minute. Add cheese and stir until melted. Add salt and pepper, to taste.

Stir-Fry Scallops or Shrimp With Cashews

Sauce:

2 T dry sherry
$\frac{1}{4}$ C ketchup
2 T oyster sauce

$\frac{1}{2}$ tsp sesame oil
$1\frac{1}{2}$ tsp rice vinegar

Cornstarch Mixture:

1 tsp cornstarch

1 tsp cold water

Stir-Fry Mixture:

2 tsp canola oil
2 cloves garlic, minced
$1\frac{1}{2}$ tsp ginger, minced
$\frac{1}{2}$ C cashews, toasted and chopped

1 to $1\frac{1}{2}$ lbs sea scallops or
   peeled raw shrimp
3 scallions, finely sliced

Combine sauce ingredients and set aside. In another small bowl, combine cornstarch and water and set aside. Heat a wok or skillet over high heat. When pan is hot, add the oil, garlic and ginger and cook for about 45 seconds. Add scallops or shrimp and stir-fry for 4 to 5 minutes, or until almost cooked. Add sauce mixture and bring to a boil. Add cornstarch mixture and cook for 1 minute. Sprinkle cashews and scallions on top. Serve over rice.

Hint: *Red wine vinegar can be substituted for rice wine vinegar.*

MEAT

Steak Kew

1 lb flank or sirloin steak, sliced across
  the grain into small strips
2 to 3 T canola oil, divided
1 T ginger, minced
2 cloves garlic, minced

1 to 2 T water (optional)
2 scallions, sliced
1 to $1\frac{1}{2}$ lbs vegetables such as broccoli,
  peppers, mushrooms or combination

Marinade:

$\frac{1}{2}$ C ketchup
2 T hoisin sauce
1 T sugar

2 T dry sherry
2 T soy sauce

Gravy:

$\frac{1}{4}$ C chicken broth
2 T cornstarch

$\frac{1}{4}$ C water

Combine marinade ingredients and add meat. Refrigerate for several hours. To cook, heat 1 to 2 tablespoons of the oil in a wok or large skillet and add ginger and garlic. Cook for 1 minute. Add marinated beef and stir-fry until it is no longer pink. Remove beef from pan. Add remaining oil and stir-fry the vegetables until they are tender-crisp. Return meat to the pan and stir-fry for 1 minute. Whisk the gravy ingredients together and add to the pan. Stir-fry until the meat is completely cooked and sauce has thickened. Serve over rice or Chinese noodles.

Hint: *When adding the vegetables to the wok, 1 tablespoon of oil may not be enough for stir-frying them. To avoid adding more oil, add 1 to 2 tablespoons water, or more, as needed.*

■ ■

Moussaka Torte

1 long eggplant
Salt, for sprinkling on eggplant
2 eggs, divided
2 T water
$\frac{1}{2}$ to 1 tsp sugar
1 to 2 T olive oil
2 large onions, diced

1 to $1\frac{1}{4}$ lb ground beef
$\frac{1}{4}$ C pignoli (pine) nuts
$\frac{1}{2}$ to 1 tsp salt
Pepper, to taste
$\frac{1}{2}$ tsp cinnamon, to taste
2 T chopped parsley
Parsley sprigs, for garnish

Peel eggplant and slice lengthwise into $\frac{1}{2}$-inch slices. Sprinkle with salt, place in a colander and drain for at least 30 minutes. Dry eggplant with paper towel. Beat 1 egg with water and dip eggplant into mixture. Sprinkle 1 side of each eggplant slice with a pinch of sugar. Heat oil in fry pan, add eggplant and cook on both sides until slightly browned and tender. Remove from pan. In the same pan, sauté the diced onions until soft. Add ground beef and cook until no longer pink. Beat 1 egg and add to beef mixture. Add pignoli nuts, salt, pepper, cinnamon and parsley. Drain most of the juices from fry pan. Spray an ovenproof 8- or 9-inch round casserole with nonstick cooking spray. Lay widest end of eggplant slices in pan close together so that it resembles the spokes of a wheel, covering entire bottom of casserole. The narrower end of the eggplant pieces should be hanging out of the casserole. Place meat mixture on top of eggplant. Fold in pieces of eggplant that were hanging over the edge of casserole, to cover part or all of the meat mixture. Place casserole in a 350° oven and bake for 30 to 35 minutes, or until meat mixture looks fairly dry. Remove from oven and turn casserole over onto a serving plate. Do this over the sink so that excess juices can leak into the sink. Garnish with sprigs of parsley.

Hint: *This is a delicious and beautiful dish that looks like a torte. When visiting my cousins in Israel, they served this and we all really enjoyed it. You can substitute ground turkey or chicken for the beef.*

Microwave Stuffed Peppers

4 large or 5 medium green peppers
1 lb ground beef, turkey or chicken
1 small onion, finely chopped
1 to 2 cloves garlic, minced
1 egg

1 C ketchup, divided
3 T parsley, minced (optional)
1 T Worcestershire sauce
$\frac{1}{2}$ to $\frac{3}{4}$ C cooked rice
Salt and pepper, to taste

Wash peppers and cut off the tops. Remove the seeds and membranes and turn upside-down to drain. Place ground meat, onion and garlic in a large bowl and cook on high for 3 minutes, stirring half way through, so that meat will get crumbly. Cook for an additional 2 minutes. Add remaining ingredients, reserving $\frac{1}{4}$ cup of ketchup. Fill the peppers with the meat mixture and place in a circle just large enough to hold them. Spread the remaining ketchup on top of the peppers. Cover the pan and cook on high for about 10 to 11 minutes, or until peppers are tender.

Hint: *A round or oval casserole dish with a cover would be ideal for cooking this dish. Otherwise, use wax paper to cover the peppers when cooking.*

Microwave Sloppy Joes

$\frac{3}{4}$ lb ground beef, turkey or chicken
$\frac{3}{4}$ C onion, diced
8 oz can tomato sauce
1 T sweet pickle relish
1 tsp brown sugar
1 T cider vinegar

1 tsp Worcestershire sauce
1 tsp prepared mustard
2 hamburger buns, split in half
2 slices Cheddar or American
    cheese, cut into 4 strips each

In a microwaveable plastic colander, combine beef, turkey or chicken and onion. Set colander in a microwaveable bowl. Microwave on high for 4 to 5 minutes, or until meat is no longer pink, stirring several times during cooking. In a $1\frac{1}{2}$-quart microwave dish, combine meat mixture, tomato sauce, pickle relish, brown sugar, vinegar, Worcestershire sauce and mustard. Microwave on high for 2 to 3 minutes, or until heated through. Spoon beef mixture evenly over 4 roll halves. Crisscross 2 cheese strips on each.

Hint: *This may also be served over pasta or rice.*

■ ■

Microwave Meat Loaf

1 lb ground beef
1 egg
$\frac{1}{3}$ C bread crumbs
$\frac{1}{4}$ C ketchup

2 T water
Garlic powder, to taste
Salt and pepper, to taste

In a medium bowl, combine all ingredients. Shape into a loaf. Place in a microwave dish.

Topping:

2 T ketchup
1 T water

1 small onion, sliced

Whisk together ketchup and water. Pour over meat loaf. Place onion slices on top. Cover with wax paper and microwave on high for 14 to 15 minutes, or until desired doneness is reached. Let stand for 5 minutes before slicing.

Hint: *You can slice leftovers and use them for sandwiches, or freeze in individual portions for future meals. If you prefer, you can bake the meat loaf in a conventional oven at 350° for 1 hour.*

Unstuffed Cabbage

1 lb ground beef, turkey or chicken
1 medium onion, chopped
1 C raw rice
26 to 28 oz spaghetti sauce
6 C green or Savoy cabbage, shredded

$1\frac{1}{4}$ C water
Salt and pepper, to taste
Grated Parmesan cheese,
    for garnish (optional)

Cook the ground meat and onion in a large pot, stirring occasionally until no longer pink. Add the rice, spaghetti sauce, cabbage and water. Cover and bring to a boil. Lower heat and simmer for 20 to 25 minutes, or until rice and cabbage are tender. Sprinkle with Parmesan cheese, if desired.

Hint: *This 1-dish meal can easily be prepared in advance and reheated. However, if you prefer to cook it immediately you can save time by chopping and shredding the cabbage a day in advance and refrigerating until needed.*

Bahme (Indonesian Stir-Fry)

1 T canola oil
1 lb ground beef, turkey or chicken
4 cloves garlic, minced
1 large onion, diced
4 stalks celery, diced

1 small green cabbage, shredded
$\frac{1}{3}$ to $\frac{1}{2}$ C soy sauce, or to taste
6 to 7 oz spaghetti, cooked and drained
Salt and pepper, to taste

Heat oil in a fry pan or wok over high heat and add meat. Add garlic, onion and celery and cook until veggies are slightly tender and meat is no longer pink. Remove meat and veggies from the pan and add cabbage and soy sauce. Stir-fry until the cabbage is wilted. Add meat mixture and spaghetti and stir until well mixed. If necessary, add more soy sauce.

Hint: This recipe, an adaptation of an Indonesian dish, is an unusual combination of flavors and textures that makes a wonderful 1-dish meal. It is high in fiber and is a good way to utilize leftover spaghetti.

Holiday Brisket

4 to 5 lbs beef brisket
1 large onion, sliced
3 to 4 carrots, sliced
1 clove garlic, minced

1 envelope dry onion soup mix
1 C ketchup
12 oz ginger ale or beer
4 to 5 potatoes, quartered

Place onion, carrots and garlic on the bottom of a large pot or roasting pan. Place brisket on top of veggies. Combine remaining ingredients, except potatoes, and pour over meat. Add potatoes. Bake at 350° for 3 to $3\frac{1}{2}$ hours, or until well-browned and tender. Baste often with pan juices. Cool slightly and then refrigerate. When cold, remove meat from refrigerator and slice thinly against the grain. To serve, heat with gravy and vegetables.

Hint: This tastes best if it is made 1 or 2 days before serving. If you prefer, it can be cooked on top of the stove.

Stifado (Greek Stew)

1 T olive oil
2 lbs stew beef
1 lb small white onions, peeled or
  1 lb frozen small boiling onions or
  1 lb yellow onions, sliced
6 oz tomato paste
$\frac{1}{2}$ C red wine
2 T red wine vinegar

2 T brown sugar
2 cloves garlic, finely minced
1 bay leaf
1 small or $\frac{1}{2}$ large cinnamon stick
$\frac{1}{4}$ tsp ground cloves
$\frac{1}{4}$ tsp cumin
$\frac{1}{4}$ C raisins or currants
Salt and pepper, to taste

Heat oil in a large pot and add meat. Stir meat with oil, but do not brown. Place onions over meat. Combine tomato paste, wine, vinegar, brown sugar and garlic and pour over onions and meat. Spread the bay leaf, cinnamon stick, cloves, cumin and raisins or currants over the top. Bring the stew to a boil. Cover and reduce heat so that it cooks at a very low simmer for 2 to 3 hours, or until meat is very tender. Do not stir meat as it cooks but adjust heat so that it keeps cooking, but doesn't burn. Remove cinnamon stick and bay leaf before serving.

Hint: *This is delicious served over rice, orzo or potatoes.*

Chinese All-Purpose Marinade

3 to 4 lbs chicken, quartered or cut into eighths or 3 lbs sirloin or flank steak

Marinade:

10 oz soy sauce
$\frac{1}{3}$ C brown sugar
3 to 4 cloves garlic, finely minced

1 tsp fresh ginger, finely
  minced or $\frac{1}{2}$ tsp powdered ginger

Combine all ingredients, except chicken or beef. Pour marinade over chicken or beef and marinate for at least 2 hours or overnight. Bake chicken at 350° for 1 hour, basting occasionally. Turn broiler on for the last few minutes to brown chicken. If using beef, broil or grill until cooked to desired doneness.

Hint: *You can make quick and delicious hors d'oeuvres by marinating thin strips of chicken or beef and then threading them onto skewers and broiling or grilling. One-third of the marinade mixture is enough for 1 pound boneless chicken breasts or 1 pound beef.*

Marinated Flank Steak

1 to 1½ lbs flank steak
2 cloves garlic, minced
2 T hoisin sauce

2 to 3 T honey
2 to 3 T soy sauce
2 T white or cider vinegar

Lay steak on a cutting board, and using a sharp knife, lightly score the steak in a cross hatch pattern on both sides. This prevents steak from curling and allows marinade flavor to permeate meat. In a large low pan, whisk together all ingredients except steak. Place steak in the pan and turn to coat both sides. Cover pan with plastic wrap or transfer steak and marinade to a plastic bag. Refrigerate for at least 5 to 6 hours or up to a day. Grill or broil steak for about 5 minutes on each side, turning often and basting with any extra marinade. When done, remove from heat and let sit for 5 minutes before slicing on the diagonal.

Hint: This marinade is also delicious with chicken. You may want to double this recipe because leftovers, combined with grilled vegetables or salad greens, make a wonderful salad or sandwich.

Spicy Crusted London Broil

2 to 2½ lbs London broil

Spice Mixture:

1 T chili powder
1 tsp paprika
1 tsp cumin

¼ tsp black pepper
⅛ tsp cinnamon

Combine all of the seasonings in a small dish. If desired, set aside 1½ teaspoons of the mixture to be used in a marinade for grilled vegetables. Place meat on a piece of wax paper or foil and rub each side with the spice mixture. Let stand at room temperature for 15 minutes, or up to 24 hours in the refrigerator. Grill or broil on both sides until meat has reached desired doneness. Let stand for 10 minutes before slicing at an angle against the grain.

Hint: Leftovers make great-tasting sandwiches! The spice mixture can also be used on other cuts of beef.

Stir-Fry Beef With Vegetables

1 lb flank or sirloin tip steak, sliced into small strips across the grain
1 to 2 T canola oil
2 cloves garlic, minced
2 medium onions, sliced

1 to 2 T water
Pea pods, small bunch broccoli, red pepper or mushrooms or any combination of 1 to $1\frac{1}{2}$ lbs fresh vegetables

Marinade:

$\frac{1}{2}$ C chicken broth
$\frac{1}{4}$ C soy sauce
2 T dry sherry, white wine or water

1 T Worcestershire sauce
1 T brown sugar
1 T cornstarch

Combine marinade ingredients in a bowl or plastic bag. Add meat and refrigerate for at least 2 hours or up to 2 days, stirring occasionally. To cook, heat oil over high heat in a wok or large pan and add garlic and onions, stir-frying for 1 to 2 minutes. Using a slotted spoon, remove meat from the marinade and reserve marinade. Stir-fry beef on high until it is no longer pink. Remove it from the wok. Add the water and vegetables to the wok and stir-fry until they are tender-crisp, about 2 to 3 minutes. Return meat and reserved marinade to the wok and cook for 1 to 2 minutes, or until the meat is completely cooked and sauce has thickened. Serve over rice or Chinese noodles.

Hint: *To reduce sodium, use low sodium soy sauce and low sodium Worcestershire sauce. Use whatever variety and amounts of veggies you like.*

Sausage Pizza Loaf

1 lb Italian sausage
16 oz spaghetti sauce

16 oz loaf Italian bread
$\frac{3}{4}$ lb Mozzarella cheese, shredded

Brown sausage in skillet. Drain well. Mix with spaghetti sauce. Cut the bread in half, lengthwise, and remove some of the insides. Top each half with sausage-sauce mixture. Place on a cookie sheet. Bake for 20 minutes at 325°. Top each half with 6 ounces Mozzarella. Place 6 inches from the broiler for 2 to 4 minutes, or until slightly brown and bubbly. Cool briefly, then slice.

Hint: *You can substitute turkey or chicken sausage for Italian pork sausage.*

■ ■

Sausage and Rice Casserole

1 lb pork, turkey or chicken sausage
2 large onions, diced
1 C raw rice
1 tsp oregano
$\frac{1}{2}$ tsp garlic powder
$\frac{1}{2}$ C water

$14\frac{1}{2}$ oz can whole peeled tomatoes,
  mashed, with juice
$1\frac{1}{2}$ C Mozzarella or Cheddar cheese
  or combination, shredded
1 medium green pepper, diced

Precook sausages by boiling for a few minutes and draining or cooking in microwave. To microwave, place sausage in a circular pattern around outside edge of a plate. Cook on high for $1\frac{1}{2}$ minutes. Turn sausage over and cook on high for another $1\frac{1}{2}$ minutes. Drain and slice into 1-inch pieces. Sprinkle rice over the bottom of a greased 2-quart casserole. Place sausage slices and onions on top of rice. Sprinkle with oregano and garlic powder. Pour tomatoes and their juice over rice mixture. Add water. Sprinkle cheese and green pepper on top. Cover tightly. Bake at 350° for $1\frac{1}{2}$ hours.

Hint: *This is an easy 1-dish meal. If you use turkey or chicken sausage, it is low in fat.*

Chinese-Style Pork Chops

1 to $1\frac{1}{2}$ lbs center-cut boneless
  pork chops
Nonstick cooking spray
1 to 2 tsp olive or canola oil
Salt and pepper, to taste
3 T ketchup
2 T rice vinegar

$1\frac{1}{2}$ T soy sauce
1 T fresh ginger, chopped
  (1" long x $\frac{1}{2}$" wide)
4 cloves garlic, minced
$\frac{1}{2}$ tsp Chinese 5 spice powder
$\frac{1}{4}$ C water

Trim all visible fat from pork chops. Season with salt and pepper. Spray a fry pan with nonstick spray. Add oil and heat until oil is hot. Add pork chops. Cook over medium heat until brown on both sides. While pork is cooking, combine all remaining ingredients in a food processor or blender and purée until smooth. Add this mixture to browned chops and bring to a boil. Reduce heat and cover. Cook for 10 to 15 minutes, or until chops are cooked to desired doneness. Serve with rice.

Hint: *This recipe is also delicious using boneless chicken breasts or turkey cutlets, however, reduce cooking time so that the chicken or turkey doesn't get tough.*

Saucy Spareribs

$1\frac{1}{2}$ C ketchup
$\frac{3}{4}$ C brown sugar
$\frac{1}{2}$ C vinegar
1 onion, chopped

$\frac{1}{4}$ C Worcestershire sauce
1 T prepared mustard
2 T chili powder
3 to 5 lbs spareribs

To make the sauce, combine all the ingredients, except spareribs. Place the spareribs in a single layer in a baking pan. Brown in the oven at 350° for 15 to 20 minutes. Drain off fat. Pour the sauce over the meat, coating each piece. Bake, covered, at 350° for 45 minutes. Remove the cover and baste the meat with the sauce. Bake an additional 15 to 20 minutes, or until meat has reached desired doneness.

Hint: *This sauce is also wonderful on chicken.*

Balsamic-Marinated Ribs

$1\frac{1}{2}$ to 2 lbs boneless ribs or
  2 beef or pork racks
$\frac{3}{4}$ C balsamic vinegar

$\frac{1}{2}$ C brown sugar
2 tsp cayenne pepper
Dash salt

In a shallow pan large enough to hold the ribs, combine all ingredients, except ribs. Whisk until the sugar dissolves. Place the ribs in the pan and turn so that both sides are covered with the marinade. Cover and refrigerate for several hours or overnight, turning the ribs several times. To cook, cover and bake at 350°, turning occasionally, for 30 to 35 minutes for boneless ribs or 45 to 55 minutes for racks, or until the meat reaches desired doneness. Remove the cover during the last 10 minutes of cooking.

Pork Chops Dijon

6 thin sliced pork chops
3 to 4 T seasoned bread crumbs

1 T freshly grated Parmesan cheese
2 to 3 tsp Dijon mustard

Combine bread crumbs and Parmesan cheese in a shallow bowl. Spread mustard on both sides of pork chops and press each chop into crumb mixture. Place on a greased broiler pan and broil chops for about 10 minutes per side, or until completely cooked. Timing depends on thickness of chops.

Hint: *Watch this carefully so that the chops don't dry out or burn!*

■ ■

Pork Medallions

$\frac{3}{4}$ to I lb pork tenderloin
I tsp sesame oil
2 cloves garlic, minced
Dash cayenne pepper

2 T water
3 T dry sherry
2 T hoisin sauce

Trim fat from tenderloin. Slice into 8 pieces. Place each piece between 2 sheets of wax paper or plastic wrap and, using a pounder, flatten to $\frac{1}{2}$ inch thickness. Spray a large fry pan with nonstick cooking spray. Add sesame oil and place over medium high heat until hot. Add garlic and cayenne pepper and sauté for I minute. Add pork and cook for 4 minutes on each side, or until done. Remove medallions from pan and keep warm. Add water, sherry and hoisin sauce to pan. Mix well with a whisk and cook for I minute, stirring constantly, or until thickened. Pour sauce over pork.

Hint: *This is low in fat and cholesterol. It is delicious served over rice.*

Caramelized Pork Tenderloin Slices

$\frac{3}{4}$ to I lb pork tenderloin, cut
  into $\frac{1}{2}$" slices
2 tsp canola or olive oil (optional)
2 cloves garlic, minced

2 T brown sugar
I T orange juice
I T molasses
Salt and pepper, to taste

Heat oil or spray nonstick cooking spray in a fry pan over medium heat. Add pork and garlic and cook for 5 to 7 minutes, turning occasionally, until pork is slightly pink in the center. Stir in remaining ingredients and cook just until mixture thickens slightly and coats the pork.

Hint: *This recipe offers a new and speedy way to prepare lean and tasty pork tenderloin. It takes only 10 minutes from start to finish!*

Herbed Pork Tenderloin
With Oven Roasted Potatoes

2 T olive oil
2 garlic cloves, minced
I tsp rosemary
I tsp thyme

Salt and pepper, to taste
$\frac{3}{4}$ to I lb pork tenderloin
3 to 4 medium potatoes, cut
    into sixths or eighths

Combine oil and seasonings and pour into a roasting pan. Place tenderloin in the pan and turn until all sides are coated. Add potatoes and, using a spoon, toss them around the pan so that they are also coated. Place the potato pieces around the meat. Roast pork at 375° for 40 to 45 minutes, or until thermometer reaches 170° and juices run clear, stirring potatoes every 15 minutes. If it is not as brown as you'd like, place pan under the broiler for about 5 minutes. Let meat stand for 5 minutes before slicing.

Hint: *To save time, roast additional vegetables in another pan while pork and potatoes are cooking.*

Grilled Pork Tenderloin

$\frac{3}{4}$ to I lb pork tenderloin
2 T hoisin sauce

2 T soy sauce
2 T honey

Whisk hoisin sauce, soy sauce and honey together and pour over meat. Marinate for a minimum of 2 hours. Grill or broil, turning often, until outside is somewhat crispy and desired doneness is reached.

Hint: *This marinade is also wonderful on beef or chicken.*

■ ■

Rack of Lamb

Rack of lamb (14 to 16 rib chops,
   divided into 2 racks)
1 T olive oil
Salt and pepper
2 T Dijon mustard

1 C fresh bread crumbs
$\frac{1}{4}$ C parsley, finely chopped
1 clove garlic, finely chopped
2 to 3 T butter, melted

To prepare the racks, cut along the length of each rib section about 1 inch below the rib eye and remove all the fat beneath it right down to the bone. Separate and clean the bones. Brush the meat with olive oil. Place the racks in a roasting pan with the rib bones of each rack facing up and crisscrossing each other. Roast at 400° for 20 minutes. While racks are cooking, prepare crumb coating by combining bread crumbs, parsley and garlic. Then remove the racks from the oven and sprinkle with salt and pepper and brush with mustard. Pat the crumb mixture on the mustard-coated racks. Drizzle with melted butter. Return meat to the oven and roast, uncovered, for 25 minutes, or until a thermometer reads 175°. For well-done lamb, cook longer. If bread crumbs get too brown during cooking, cover the racks with foil. Let the lamb sit for about 10 minutes before serving.

Hint: *This is an elegant but easy recipe that is perfect for "special guests" or people you want to impress! When figuring out how many racks to buy, plan on at least 3 or 4 rib chops per person. To make it really fancy, you can purchase frilly white papers to put on the ends of the chops!*

Grilled Spiced Lamb Kabobs

2 lbs lamb steaks or roast, cut
   into 2" cubes
1 medium onion, minced
2 T lemon juice
$\frac{1}{2}$ tsp thyme

1 to 2 T olive oil
1 green pepper, cut into 2" cubes
1 red pepper, cut into 2" cubes
24 cherry tomatoes
Salt and pepper, to taste

Place lamb in a bowl. Add onion, lemon juice, thyme and olive oil. Toss well. Cover and marinate for a minimum of 2 hours or up to 24 hours. When ready to grill, remove lamb from the marinade and place on skewers, alternating with peppers and tomatoes. Grill over moderate heat, turning every 3 to 4 minutes, until the meat is cooked to desired doneness. Add salt and pepper, to taste. Serve over rice or in pita bread.

Hint: *The kabobs can be broiled instead of grilled.*

Veal Paprikash

1 tsp olive or canola oil
2 lbs boneless veal, cut into
  $1\frac{1}{2}$ to 2" cubes
1 medium onion, diced
1 T paprika
$\frac{1}{8}$ tsp cayenne pepper

$14\frac{1}{2}$ oz can whole or chopped
  tomatoes, with juice
$\frac{1}{2}$ C chicken broth or water
$\frac{1}{4}$ to $\frac{1}{3}$ C sour cream
Salt and pepper, to taste

Heat oil in a large saucepan. Add veal and lightly brown on all sides. Add onions and cook until golden. Add paprika and cayenne pepper, tomatoes and broth or water. Bring to a boil, cover pan and then reduce heat. Simmer for 1 hour or until veal is tender. Season to taste. Just before serving, add sour cream and stir until it is well blended with the sauce. Heat gently, but do not boil. Serve over noodles or rice.

Hint: *To reduce fat, use light sour cream. If you really want a minimum amount of fat, use nonfat yogurt. It will be tasty but not as authentic tasting as with sour cream. Also, refrigerate paprika so that it will maintain its flavor and color.*

Veal Cacciatore

1 lb boneless veal cubes
1 C tomato purée
$\frac{1}{2}$ C water
1 large onion, sliced
1 C chicken broth
1 clove garlic, minced

$\frac{1}{2}$ tsp basil
$\frac{1}{2}$ tsp oregano
Fresh black pepper, to taste
2 large green peppers, sliced
1 C mushrooms, sliced

Brown veal in a nonstick skillet or a pan sprayed with nonstick spray. Add remaining ingredients except peppers and mushrooms. Cover and cook over low heat for 45 minutes. Add peppers and mushrooms and cook for an additional 10 minutes. Serve over noodles.

POULTRY

Orange Skillet Chicken

2 to 3 whole chicken breasts, split, or
  I whole chicken, quartered
2 tsp olive or canola oil
6 oz can frozen orange juice
  concentrate, defrosted

3 T ketchup
Rind of I orange, grated
I I oz can mandarin oranges,
  drained, for garnish

Place oil in a large skillet or electric fry pan. When oil is hot, add chicken and cook until golden on both sides. Combine orange juice concentrate, ketchup and orange rind. Pour over chicken. Cover skillet and cook over low-medium heat for 40 to 45 minutes, or until chicken is tender and completely cooked. Add mandarin oranges, if desired. Serve over rice or baked potato.

Hint: *To reduce fat, remove the skin of the chicken before cooking.*

Chicken Picadillo

3 to 4 lbs chicken, cut into quarters
I to 2 T olive or canola oil
I onion, chopped
$14\frac{1}{2}$ oz can whole tomatoes, chopped
$\frac{1}{2}$ tsp cumin
$\frac{1}{2}$ C golden raisins

Dash cayenne pepper
$1\frac{1}{2}$ T chopped green chilies
I tsp sugar
I tsp cinnamon
$\frac{1}{4}$ C almonds, sliced

Heat oil in a large fry pan or large pot. Add chicken and cook for about 10 minutes, turning so that all sides are golden. Add onion and cook for 2 to 3 additional minutes, or until slightly tender. Combine all remaining ingredients, except almonds, and add to chicken. Cover the pan and cook over low heat for 35 minutes. Uncover and cook for 5 to 10 more minutes, or until chicken reaches desired doneness. Sprinkle with almonds. Serve over rice.

Roast Chicken With Caribbean Spice Rub

3 to 4 lb whole roasting chicken
2 large onions, sliced
Juice of 1 lemon
1 tsp salt
1 tsp black pepper

2 tsp dry mustard
1 tsp cinnamon
1 tsp garlic powder
1 tsp water, or more, as needed
$1\frac{1}{2}$ C chicken broth

Place onions in a roasting pan. Place chicken, breast-side down, on top of the onions. Rub lemon juice into the chicken. Combine all the spices in a small bowl. Add the water, a little at a time, until a paste is formed. Rub this paste onto the skin of the chicken. Bake at 425° for 30 minutes. Turn chicken over and reduce heat to 375°. Pour broth over the chicken. Roast for 1 hour longer, basting every 10 minutes. Let chicken sit for 10 minutes before carving.

Hint: *This chicken is not as spicy as it sounds. Although I usually don't cook with so much salt, it is needed in this recipe. The chicken is very moist and forms a gravy which is delicious over rice, potatoes or noodles.*

Honey and Garlic Chicken

5 to 7 lb chicken or capon
$\frac{1}{4}$ C water
2 to 3 tsp paprika
$\frac{1}{2}$ C honey

$\frac{1}{4}$ C ketchup
2 cloves garlic, minced
$\frac{1}{4}$ C soy sauce
2 T brown sugar

Place chicken in a roasting pan. Pour water into pan. Sprinkle chicken with paprika. Roast, uncovered, at 350° for 30 minutes. While chicken cooks, combine remaining ingredients in a saucepan and heat until well blended. Pour this sauce over the chicken and then cover the pan with foil. Roast for 45 minutes, basting occasionally. Uncover and roast for 15 additional minutes, or until chicken reaches desired doneness, basting once or twice.

Hint: *For an easy meal, bake potatoes or rice in the oven while the chicken is cooking.*

■ ■

Honey-Glazed Chicken With Apples

1 chicken, quartered
Salt and pepper, to taste
Garlic powder, to taste
4 apples, cored, peeled and sliced
$\frac{1}{4}$ C apple juice or cider

$\frac{1}{4}$ C honey
1 T brown sugar
Rind of 1 lemon, grated
Rind of 1 orange, grated
$\frac{1}{4}$ C orange marmalade

Place the chicken in a roasting pan. Sprinkle with salt, pepper and garlic powder. Place the apples around the edges of the pan. Roast at 350° for 40 minutes. Drain the accumulated liquid and discard. In a small pot, combine the apple juice or cider, honey, brown sugar, lemon and orange rind and heat until the honey is dissolved. Baste the chicken and apples with this mixture. Bake for 10 to 15 minutes longer, basting every 5 minutes, until the chicken is golden. Brush orange marmalade over the chicken and apples and bake for an additional 5 to 10 minutes. If not as brown as you would like, put chicken under the broiler for a few minutes.

Hint: This recipe is perfect in the fall and winter when apples and cider are plentiful. It is even more delicious if you make it a day in advance and reheat it.

Garlic Broiled Chicken

1 chicken, cut in quarters
2 to 3 tsp Lawry's seasoned salt

1 tsp garlic powder

Remove skin and as much fat as possible from chicken. Wash chicken and dry with paper towels. Place "skin-side" down (even though skin has been removed) on broiler pan. Sprinkle with half the seasoned salt and half the garlic powder. Place 3 to 4 inches below broiling element in oven and broil for about 15 minutes. Turn chicken over and sprinkle with remaining seasoned salt and garlic powder. Continue broiling for about 20 to 25 minutes, checking to make sure chicken doesn't burn. You may have to turn chicken pieces quite frequently or place broiling pan a little lower from heat source so it doesn't burn or dry out the chicken. If chicken is not completely cooked inside, but is brown enough on the outside, reduce oven to 350° and bake for an additional 10 to 15 minutes.

Hint: For best results, be sure to turn the chicken often. This recipe is my youngest son's favorite!

■ ■

Epicurean Chicken

2 to 3 lbs chicken breasts, split
$\frac{3}{4}$ C rosé or white wine
$\frac{1}{4}$ C soy sauce
1 tsp ginger
$\frac{3}{4}$ C chicken broth

1 T brown sugar
3 cloves garlic, minced
$\frac{1}{2}$ tsp oregano
2 T cornstarch

Place chicken in a greased roasting pan or casserole. Combine remaining ingredients and whisk well. Pour over chicken. Cover with foil or lid of casserole dish. Bake at 375° for 45 minutes. Turn chicken over and bake, covered, for 15 minutes. Uncover and baste with pan juices. Bake for 15 additional minutes, basting occasionally.

Peking Chicken

1 lb boneless chicken breast
(16) 6" flour tortillas

1 bunch scallions, sliced
1 C hoisin sauce

Marinade:

4 T soy sauce
2 tsp lemon juice
2 cloves garlic, minced

1 T ginger, minced
$\frac{1}{4}$ tsp paprika
1 T sesame seeds

Combine ingredients for marinade in a pie plate. Add chicken and turn so that it is well coated. Marinate for a minimum of 1 hour, preferably longer. When ready to cook, place chicken around the edges of the pie plate, with the thickest portions of the breasts towards the outside of the pan. Lay 1 piece of white paper towel over pie plate; do not tuck in. Microwave on high, turning once, for 5 to 6 minutes, or until chicken is no longer pink. Check to make sure chicken is completely cooked. However, do not overbake or chicken will be tough. To heat the tortillas, stack several together and wrap loosely in a paper towel. Microwave on high for 1 to 2 minutes, or until hot. While tortillas are heating, slice chicken thinly and place on a platter. Place hoisin sauce in 1 bowl and scallions in another. To serve, spread some hoisin sauce on a tortilla and add scallions and chicken. Roll up and eat with your hands.

Hint*: This recipe is an adaptation of traditional Peking duck. Chicken is used instead of duck and tortillas are a substitute for Peking pancakes.*

Mom's "Red Chicken"

3 to 4 lbs chicken, quartered
1 T olive oil
2 large onions, sliced
1 C ketchup
1½ C water

12 sun dried tomatoes, sliced
  in half (optional)
24 mini-carrots or ½ lb carrots,
  peeled and sliced
Salt and pepper, to taste

Heat oil in a large pot. Place chicken pieces in a large pot and sear briefly on each side until they just start to take on a little color. Add onions, ketchup and water. Cover pan and bring to a boil. Reduce heat and add sun dried tomatoes and carrots. Turn heat down and simmer for 45 minutes to 1 hour, or until chicken is tender. Check pan occasionally to make sure there is enough liquid in the pan, adding more ketchup or water, as needed. Season with salt and pepper. Serve over noodles.

Hint: "Red Chicken" is the name my niece and nephew have given to one of their Grandma's favorite recipes. To make this healthier, remove the skin from the chicken before cooking.

Orange Chicken

3 to 4 lbs chicken, cut up
⅓ C flour

Salt, pepper and paprika, to taste
1 to 2 T canola or olive oil

Sauce:

6 oz frozen orange juice
  concentrate, thawed
6 oz water
3 heaping T brown sugar

1 T vinegar
1 T basil
½ tsp ginger

Mix flour and seasonings together and place in a plastic bag. Shake chicken in the bag just until coated. Remove chicken and sauté in oil until it becomes light brown in color. Remove from skillet and transfer to a roasting pan. Combine sauce ingredients and pour over chicken. Bake at 350° for 45 minutes, or until tender.

Hint: If you are trying to keep the fat content as low as possible you can skip sautéing the chicken and just bake it for about 1 hour. Also, removing the skin before cooking the chicken eliminates most of the fat.

■ ■

Cantonese Chicken

3 to 4 lbs chicken quarters
6 Chinese dried mushrooms
4 cloves garlic, finely minced, divided
4 thin slices ginger
1 tsp sugar
2 T cornstarch
4 T soy sauce

2 T oyster sauce
2 T dry sherry
1 tsp sesame oil
1 to 2 tsp canola oil
1 scallion, cut into 1" pieces
1 chopped scallion, for garnish

Soak mushrooms in hot water for at least 30 minutes, or until soft. Drain, remove stems and cut into thin slices. Set aside. Clean chicken and remove skin, if desired. Cut into 2-inch pieces, keeping bones attached. In a large bowl, whisk together 2 of the cloves of garlic, ginger, sugar, cornstarch, soy sauce, oyster sauce, sherry and sesame oil. Add chicken and mix so that all chicken pieces are well coated. Marinate for at least 30 minutes in the refrigerator. To cook, heat 1 to 2 teaspoons canola oil in a large pot. Add remaining 2 cloves of minced garlic and scallion pieces and stir-fry for 2 minutes. Add marinated chicken and stir to coat all pieces. Cover and cook over medium heat for 30 minutes, stirring occasionally. Add mushrooms and cook 10 more minutes, or until desired doneness is reached. Garnish with chopped scallions.

Hint: *Although this is rather messy to eat, it has a really succulent taste that I am sure you will enjoy. Removing the skin before cooking reduces the fat.*

Crock Pot BBQ Chicken

2 chickens, cut into quarters (8 pieces)
1 onion, sliced

18 oz BBQ sauce of your choice

Place chicken in the bottom of the crock pot. Cover with onion slices and sauce. Cover and cook on low for 6 to 8 hours, or until tender.

Hint: *This easy and delicious recipe is very healthy, especially if you use all chicken breasts and remove the skin before cooking. The gravy is wonderful over rice or pasta.*

Southwestern White Chili

1 lb boneless chicken breasts, cut
  into $\frac{1}{2}$" cubes
2 tsp olive oil
1 small onion, diced
1 C chicken broth
4 oz can chopped green
  chilies, undrained
1 tsp garlic powder
1 tsp cumin

$\frac{1}{2}$ tsp oregano
1 T fresh cilantro, minced
Dash cayenne pepper
19 oz can cannellini (white kidney)
  beans, undrained
2 scallions, sliced
1 C Monterey Jack cheese,
  shredded (garnish)

Heat oil in a saucepan and add onion and chicken. Sauté for 5 minutes, stirring occasionally. Add broth, chilies and spices. Bring to a boil. Immediately reduce to simmer. Cover and simmer for 15 to 20 minutes. Stir in beans and simmer for 5 to 10 minutes. Top with scallions. Garnish with cheese, if desired. This may be served over rice or couscous.

Hint: Fresh or frozen cilantro is wonderful to keep on hand. Cut off just the thick ends of the stems and discard. Wash and thoroughly dry the remainder of the bunch. Chop it finely by hand or in the food processor. It will keep in a plastic bag or container in the refrigerator for several days, or in the freezer for months.

Chicken Pizzaiola

1 lb boneless chicken breast
1 egg, beaten
$\frac{1}{3}$ to $\frac{1}{2}$ C seasoned bread crumbs
1 T olive oil
$\frac{1}{4}$ C ketchup

$\frac{1}{4}$ tsp oregano
2 T Parmesan cheese
3 to 4 oz Mozzarella cheese,
  sliced or shredded

With a meat mallet or pounder, pound chicken breasts to $\frac{1}{2}$-inch thickness. Dip each breast into egg and then into bread crumbs. Heat oil in a fry pan and sauté chicken slowly until lightly browned on both sides. Combine ketchup and oregano and spoon 1 tablespoon of mixture over each breast. Sprinkle with Parmesan and place Mozzarella on top. Cover pan and cook for an additional 2 to 3 minutes, or until the cheese is melted.

Hint: Serve this with pasta and salad for a quick and delicious meal.

Sesame Chicken Breasts With Apricot Sauce

2 lbs boneless chicken breasts
1 C flour
3 eggs
$\frac{1}{4}$ C soy sauce
3 T water
2 C bread crumbs

$\frac{1}{2}$ C sesame seeds
$2\frac{1}{2}$ tsp paprika
$1\frac{1}{4}$ tsp garlic powder
1 tsp salt
$\frac{1}{2}$ tsp pepper
3 to 4 T canola or olive oil

Pound chicken breasts until they are about $\frac{1}{3}$ inch thick. Place flour on a piece of wax paper. In a shallow bowl, combine eggs, soy sauce and water. On another piece of wax paper, combine bread crumbs, sesame seeds, paprika, garlic powder, salt and pepper. Dredge each piece of chicken first in flour, then in egg mixture and then in crumb mixture. Again, dip each piece of chicken in the flour, egg and crumbs. Heat oil in a large fry pan and add coated chicken, a few pieces at a time. Heat over low-medium heat just until golden on each side. Remove from fry pan and place on a greased cookie sheet. Bake at 350° for 15 to 20 minutes, or until chicken reaches desired doneness. Serve with apricot sauce.

Apricot Sauce

1 C apricot jam
1 clove garlic, minced or
   1 tsp dry minced garlic

2 to 3 tsp soy sauce
3 T water

Combine ingredients and simmer for 15 minutes or microwave on high for 3 minutes, stirring once.

Hint: In preparation to store the chicken in the freezer, sauté it until golden on each side, but do not bake. Freeze chicken on a cookie sheet. When frozen, remove from cookie sheet and place in plastic bags or containers and put back in the freezer. To serve, heat frozen chicken at 350° for 15 to 20 minutes, or until cooked to desired doneness. To use as an hors d'oeuvre, cut chicken into "finger-size" pieces, before coating and cooking. Follow above procedure, reducing baking time accordingly. This is a great dish for a party, because it can be prepared and frozen weeks in advance and heated just before serving. The sauce can be made several hours ahead and reheated.

Stir-Fry Chicken With Vegetables

Featured in Cover Photo

$\frac{3}{4}$ lb boneless chicken breasts, cut
  into $\frac{1}{2}$" cubes
2 T canola oil, divided
3 scallions, chopped

$\frac{1}{4}$ lb peapods
1 red pepper, cut into $\frac{1}{2}$" cubes
1 C mushrooms, sliced
1 to 2 T water

Gravy Mixture:

1 tsp sugar
2 tsp cornstarch

$2\frac{1}{2}$ to 3 T soy sauce
$\frac{1}{2}$ C chicken broth

Preheat wok or deep pot with 1 tablespoon of the oil. Add scallions and cook for 1 minute. Add chicken and stir-fry until it turns white and is almost completely cooked. Remove from pan. Add remaining tablespoon of oil to pan and add vegetables. Stir-fry until slightly cooked (still crisp), adding water, if needed, to prevent sticking. Put partially cooked chicken back in the pan. In a small bowl, combine the gravy ingredients and whisk together. Pour into pan and keep stir-frying until chicken is completely cooked and gravy is thickened. Serve over rice or Chinese noodles.

Hint: *This recipe is a basic formula which can be used for any other protein such as tofu, beef or seafood. Use whatever variety of vegetables you like.*

Chicken With Lemon and Soy Sauce

Featured in Cover Photo

1 lb boneless chicken breasts
1 egg white, beaten
$\frac{1}{2}$ C bread crumbs

1 to 2 T canola or olive oil
3 T lemon juice
3 to 4 T soy sauce

Pound chicken breasts until they are of uniform thickness. Dip into egg and then bread crumbs. Heat oil in a large skillet. Add chicken and sauté on both sides until almost golden. Add lemon juice and soy sauce which have been combined. Cover and cook for 5 to 10 minutes, or just until tender.

Hint: *You can also cut the chicken into small cubes. Prepare it the same way as above, except stir-frying, instead of sautéing.*

■ ■

Chicken and Barley Stew

5 C chicken broth or bouillon
$\frac{3}{4}$ C barley
I lb carrots, peeled and cut
  into 2" slices
3 stalks celery, cut into I" slices
I large onion, diced
3 cloves garlic, minced
I tsp thyme

$\frac{1}{4}$ tsp red pepper flakes
I red pepper, cut into I" cubes
I lb boneless and skinless chicken
  breast, cut into 2" chunks
2 Granny Smith, Cortland or Delicious
  apples, peeled and cut into I" chunks
Salt and pepper, to taste

Combine broth, barley, carrots, celery, onion, garlic, thyme and red pepper flakes. Bring to a boil, lower heat and cover. Simmer for 12 minutes. Stir in red pepper. Cover and simmer for 6 minutes. Add chicken and apples and cook for 6 to 8 minutes, or until chicken is cooked and barley is tender. Season with salt and pepper.

Hint: *This is a healthy I-dish meal. Baby carrots, cut in half, can be substituted for the carrot slices.*

Chicken With Artichokes

I lb boneless chicken breasts,
  cut into $1\frac{1}{2}$" pieces
2 to 3 T flour
Black pepper, to taste
I to 2 T olive oil
2 cloves garlic, minced

I tsp oregano
$13\frac{3}{4}$ oz can artichoke hearts, drained
  and cut in half
3 T lemon juice
$\frac{3}{4}$ C white wine or chicken broth
3 T parsley, chopped

Combine flour and black pepper on a piece of wax paper or in a shallow bowl. Dredge chicken pieces in this mixture. Heat the oil and garlic in a fry pan and cook until the pan is hot. Add the chicken and oregano and stir-fry for 3 to 4 minutes. Add the artichoke halves, lemon juice and wine or broth. Cover the pan and simmer for 5 to 7 minutes, or until the chicken is tender. Sprinkle with parsley.

Hint: *This tastes great over linguine or spaghetti.*

■ ■

Chicken Kiev

8 skinless and boneless
  chicken breast halves
$\frac{1}{2}$ C butter or margarine, softened
1 clove garlic, minced
2 T parsley, chopped
2 T chives or tarragon, chopped

Salt and white pepper, to taste
Few T flour
1 egg, beaten with 1 T water
1 C bread crumbs
Few T olive oil

Combine the butter or margarine and herbs. Shape into 8 elongated oval pieces and freeze. Pound chicken breasts to $\frac{1}{4}$-inch thickness. Sprinkle with salt and pepper. Place 1 of the frozen butter pieces on the center of each breast half and roll so that the butter is completely enclosed. Secure with toothpicks. Roll each chicken piece in flour, egg and then bread crumbs. Heat oil in a fry pan and sauté each piece until light golden on both sides, about 10 to 12 minutes. Transfer to a preheated 350° oven and bake for 30 to 35 minutes, or until chicken reaches desired doneness.

Hint: This is a healthier version of a classic recipe in which the chicken is deep fried at 325°, until golden, for only 5 to 7 minutes.

Microwave Chicken Parmesan

1 lb boneless chicken breasts
1 egg, beaten with 2 T water
$\frac{1}{3}$ C seasoned bread crumbs
1 T olive or canola oil, divided

1 C tomato sauce or spaghetti sauce
$\frac{1}{2}$ tsp oregano
$\frac{1}{2}$ C Mozzarella cheese, shredded

Dip chicken in egg mixture and then in bread crumbs. Place $1\frac{1}{2}$ teaspoons of the oil in a 9-inch pie plate or square pan. Place coated chicken in dish and sprinkle with remaining oil. Cook on high for 2 minutes. Turn chicken over and cook for about $2\frac{1}{2}$ minutes. Top with sauce and sprinkle with oregano. Cover with wax paper and cook for 3 to 4 minutes, or until sauce is hot and chicken is tender. Sprinkle with Mozzarella cheese and let stand, covered, for 5 minutes, or until cheese is melted.

Hint: To cook 2 pounds of chicken breasts, double everything except the egg mixture and cook in a 9"x13" pan. You may need to increase the cooking time slightly. An egg substitute can be used instead of an egg.

Turkey or Chicken Divan

$\frac{1}{2}$ to $\frac{3}{4}$ lb cooked turkey or
  chicken, sliced

$\frac{1}{2}$ to $\frac{3}{4}$ lb cooked broccoli or asparagus
2 to 3 T Parmesan cheese

Place turkey or chicken in a greased 9-inch baking dish. Arrange broccoli or asparagus on top and cover with **Mornay Sauce**. Sprinkle with Parmesan cheese. Bake at 350° for 15 to 20 minutes, or until sauce is bubbling and golden.

Mornay Sauce — conventional method:

2 T butter or margarine
2 T flour
Dash cayenne pepper

1 C warm milk
$\frac{1}{2}$ C Swiss or Parmesan cheese, grated
Salt and white pepper, to taste

Melt butter or margarine over low heat. Add flour and cayenne pepper and cook slowly, stirring continuously, for 2 to 3 minutes, or until the "roux" (mixture) of flour and butter is well blended. Gradually stir in the warm milk. Increase the heat to medium and cook, stirring continuously, until the sauce is thick and smooth. Simmer, stirring for 3 to 4 minutes. This is **Béchamel Sauce** (white sauce). Add the cheese to make Mornay sauce. Season to taste.

Mornay Sauce — microwave method:

2 T butter or margarine
2 T flour
Dash cayenne pepper

1 C milk
$\frac{1}{2}$ C Swiss or Parmesan cheese, grated
Salt and white pepper, to taste

Place the butter or margarine in a 1-quart bowl and cook on high for 40 seconds, or until completely melted. Stir in the flour and cayenne pepper. Continue cooking for 45 seconds. Add the milk slowly, beating with a whisk. Continue cooking for about 3 minutes, stirring once or twice. Add the cheese and season to taste. If you want a thicker sauce, cook it longer.

Hint: *This is a good way to recycle your leftover Thanksgiving turkey or any leftover turkey or chicken throughout the year.*

Turkey Chili

I T olive oil
I large onion, chopped
5 to 6 cloves garlic, minced
1½ to 2 lbs ground turkey
I to 1½ T chili powder
I T cumin
I T oregano
I to 1½ tsp kosher salt

(2) 28 oz cans tomatoes, crushed or
  coarsely chopped
15 to 19 oz can kidney beans,
  rinsed and drained
15 to 19 oz can black beans,
  rinsed and drained
15 to 19 oz can cannellini (white kidney)
  beans, rinsed and drained

Garnishes:

¼ C fresh basil, chopped
¼ C fresh cilantro, chopped

Juice of fresh lime

Heat the oil in a large soup pot over medium heat until hot. Add the onion and garlic and cook until golden, about 6 to 7 minutes. Add the turkey, chili powder, cumin and oregano, stirring to break up the meat. Cook until the turkey becomes light in color, about 5 to 6 minutes. Add tomatoes, beans and salt and bring to a boil. Reduce heat and simmer for about 45 minutes. Garnish with basil, cilantro and/or lime juice, if desired.

Hint: This tastes best when made a day or two in advance. Ground beef or chicken may be substituted for the turkey.

Quick and Healthy Turkey Cutlets

½ C seasoned bread crumbs
½ tsp garlic powder
I lb turkey cutlets
Few T canola or olive oil

I egg white mixed with I T water
  or skim milk
Lemon wedges, for garnish
Parsley, for garnish

Combine bread crumbs and garlic. Dip turkey into egg white mixture and then into crumbs. Refrigerate for 30 minutes so coating will stick. Heat oil in a fry pan. Add turkey and cook for 2 to 3 minutes per side. Do not overcook or turkey will be tough. Garnish with lemon wedges and parsley.

Hint: This recipe also works well with chicken or veal cutlets. The egg white or skim milk are both low cholesterol alternatives to the traditional whole egg usually used for breading.

■ ■

Duck a L'Orange

I duck	$\frac{1}{2}$ tsp onion powder
I orange, quartered	2 T honey
$\frac{1}{2}$ tsp garlic powder	I tsp Gravy Master

Place the quartered orange, garlic powder and onion powder inside the duck. Preheat the oven to 425°. Place the duck on a "V"-shaped rack (can be greased or sprayed with nonstick spray to prevent duck from sticking to it), breast side up. Reduce the oven temperature to 325° and place the duck in the oven. To get the fat out, prick the duck every 20 minutes with a fork. *Don't baste*. After 2 hours, turn the duck over. Roast for another few minutes and then brush with a mixture of honey and Gravy Master. Continue cooking, basting occasionally, until cooked to desired doneness. Serve with **Orange Sauce**.

Orange Sauce

$\frac{1}{3}$ C brown sugar	I T orange rind, grated
$\frac{1}{3}$ C sugar	I C orange juice
I T cornstarch	Pinch salt

Stir all ingredients in a saucepan over medium heat until thick and clear. Do not stop stirring or the sauce may burn. This might take quite awhile. To serve the duck, cut the breast lengthwise and then in half. Pour orange sauce over duck.

Hint: *This is delicious served with rice pilaf or wild rice.*

VEGETABLES AND POTATOES

Vegetables in Oyster Sauce

1 lb green beans, broccoli or asparagus
  or combination
2 T oyster sauce

2 to 3 T dry roasted peanuts,
  coarsely chopped

Cut off ends of string beans and cut beans in half. For broccoli, cut stems and florets into 2- to 3-inch pieces. For asparagus, cut off woody ends and cut stalks in thirds. Steam beans, broccoli or asparagus until just tender. Transfer to a large serving bowl and add oyster sauce and peanuts. Toss to combine.

Hint: *Oyster sauce is located in the Oriental section of supermarkets. Use unsalted peanuts if you don't like a very salty taste.*

Asparagus, Mushrooms and Artichokes With Bread Crumbs

$\frac{3}{4}$ to 1 lb asparagus, trimmed and
  cut into 1" pieces
8 to 10 oz mushrooms, halved
  (quartered, if large)
$13\frac{3}{4}$ oz can artichoke hearts,
  drained and halved

1 medium onion, chopped
$\frac{1}{4}$ C parsley, chopped
$\frac{1}{4}$ C seasoned bread crumbs
$\frac{1}{4}$ C olive oil
Salt and pepper, to taste

Place asparagus, mushrooms, artichokes and onion in a large skillet. Sprinkle with parsley and bread crumbs. Drizzle with olive oil and season with salt and pepper. Cover and cook on medium for 10 minutes. Uncover, stir, and turn up heat. Cook for 1 to 2 minutes, or until all the liquid has evaporated.

Garden Vegetable Casserole

$\frac{2}{3}$ C slivered almonds
1 T olive or canola oil
1 lb zucchini, sliced
1 lb eggplant, cubed
1 large onion, diced
1 T flour
2 cloves garlic, minced

2 C fresh tomatoes (2 to 3 large), diced,
   or $14\frac{1}{2}$ oz can tomatoes, undrained and
   cut into chunks
Salt and pepper, to taste
1 tsp basil
6 oz Swiss, Fontina or Cheddar
   cheese, shredded

Sauté almonds in oil. When almonds are lightly toasted, remove from skillet with slotted spoon. Add zucchini, eggplant and onion to skillet. Cover and cook over medium-low heat for 15 minutes, stirring often to prevent sticking. Mix in flour, garlic, tomatoes, salt, pepper and basil. Layer vegetable mixture, almonds, and cheese in a greased 2-quart baking dish, ending with almonds on top. To serve immediately, bake uncovered at 400° for 15 to 20 minutes, or until bubbly. To serve later, cover and refrigerate. To heat, uncover and bake at 400° for 30 to 35 minutes, or until hot and bubbly.

Hint: *This is a delicious way to use up an overflow of vegetables from your garden, your neighbor's garden or your local farmer's market or supermarket!*

Cauliflower Polonaise

1 large head cauliflower
1 C bread crumbs
$\frac{1}{2}$ C butter or margarine
3 to 4 T lemon juice

1 tsp paprika
Salt and pepper, to taste
3 to 4 T parsley, chopped (optional)

Remove outer leaves and core from cauliflower. Place cauliflower in a large saucepan with boiling water or in a vegetable steamer. Bring to a boil, lower heat and cook for 20 to 25 minutes, or until tender. Drain. Sauté bread crumbs in butter or margarine until light brown. Add lemon juice, paprika, salt, pepper and parsley and blend well. Sprinkle this mixture over the cauliflower.

Hint: *You can microwave the cauliflower in a pie plate. Add $\frac{1}{4}$ cup water, cover with plastic wrap and cook on high for 8 to 9 minutes, or until tender.*

■ ■

Capunatina

I large eggplant, diced with skin on
2 T olive oil
I large Spanish onion, coarsely chopped
3 medium fresh tomatoes, skinned and
  chopped or 14½ oz can whole
  tomatoes, coarsely chopped
I or 2 T tomato paste
I T wine vinegar
2 T pitted green olives, sliced

1½ T capers (optional)
Salt and pepper, to taste
2 T pine nuts, toasted
½ C celery, diced
½ C golden and/or dark raisins soaked
  in several changes of water for 20 min.
  to remove some of the sugar
2 T pitted black olives, sliced

In a large fry pan, brown the eggplant in olive oil over high heat, watching carefully so that it doesn't burn. Do not overcook. Remove it from the pan. In the same fry pan, sauté the onions over medium heat until they are transparent, but not brown. Add the eggplant, along with the remaining ingredients and cook over low heat, stirring occasionally, for approximately 30 minutes.

Hint: This is delicious served hot or cold as a side dish or on crackers or French bread as an hors d'oeuvre.

Grilled Vegetables

2 lbs assorted vegetables, such as portobello mushrooms, zucchini, yellow squash, peppers, eggplant or onions

Marinade:

2 T olive oil
2 T Worcestershire sauce
2 T balsamic vinegar

2 cloves garlic, minced
Salt and pepper, to taste

Combine marinade ingredients in a large bowl. Add vegetables and marinate for at least 15 to 30 minutes, or up to several hours. Drain veggies and grill, turning once, until tender.

Hint: The vegetables may be grilled in a "grill basket" so that they don't fall through the grids of the grill, or they may be wrapped in heavy aluminum foil which is folded into a "packet" and placed on the grill. Turn packet over every 5 minutes until veggies are done.

Spicy Grilled Veggies

$1\frac{1}{2}$ to 2 lbs vegetables such as long slices of zucchini, wide strips of peppers or large chunks of onion

Marinade:

$1\frac{1}{2}$ tsp spice mixture (see **Spicy Crusted London Broil** pg. 89)
$\frac{1}{2}$ C cider vinegar
$\frac{1}{2}$ C water

1 T olive or canola oil
2 tsp soy sauce
1 tsp sugar

Combine marinade ingredients and add veggies. Allow veggies to marinate for at least 1 hour, or up to 24 hours. Remove from marinade and grill or broil for 10 to 15 minutes, turning occasionally, until tender.

Mashed Parsnips

1 lb parsnips
2 garlic cloves, minced
1 to 2 T butter or margarine

$\frac{1}{2}$ C hot milk
Salt and white pepper, to taste

Peel and coarsely chop the parsnips. Place them in a saucepan and cover with water. Boil until soft, about 25 to 30 minutes. Drain well and mash with remaining ingredients. Mix thoroughly and serve hot.

Hint: *These look very similar to mashed potatoes but the taste is quite different.*

Microwave Ginger Honey Carrots

1 lb carrots
$\frac{1}{4}$ C orange juice

$\frac{1}{4}$ tsp fresh ginger, grated
1 to $1\frac{1}{2}$ tsp honey

Peel the carrots and cut into 1-inch diagonal slices. Place all ingredients in a microwaveable pan. Cover and cook on high for 3 to 4 minutes, or until carrots reach desired doneness.

Hint: *Baby carrots, which don't require peeling or slicing, work very nicely in this recipe. If you prefer not to use the microwave, you can cook this, covered, on top of the stove.*

■ ■ ■ ■ ■ ■ ■ ■ ■ ■ ■ ■ ▶ ■ ■ ■ ■ ■ ■ ■ ■ ■ ■ ■ ■ ■ ■ ■ ■ ■

Celery Sauté

8 large celery stalks
$1\frac{1}{2}$ C mushrooms, sliced

$1\frac{1}{2}$ to 2 T butter or margarine
$\frac{1}{3}$ C slivered almonds, toasted

Slice the celery diagonally into bite-size pieces. Cook in a small amount of boiling water until just crisp-tender or place the celery and 2 tablespoons water in a microwaveable dish and cook on high for $1\frac{1}{2}$ to 2 minutes, until slightly cooked, but still somewhat crisp. Drain celery. In a large fry pan, sauté mushrooms in butter or margarine until softened. Add celery and almonds. Toss and cook just until celery is hot.

Hint: To toast almonds, bake at 350° for 5 to 7 minutes, watching carefully to prevent burning.

Acorn Squash With Applesauce

2 acorn squash, halved
  lengthwise, seeds removed
2 tsp lemon juice
$\frac{1}{4}$ C raisins

$\frac{1}{4}$ C brown sugar
3 T walnuts, chopped
$1\frac{1}{2}$ C applesauce

Combine all ingredients except squash. Place the squash halves in a pan which contains $\frac{1}{2}$ inch water. Fill the halves with the applesauce mixture. Bake at 400° for 1 hour, or until the squash is tender.

Sautéed Mushrooms

2 tsp olive oil or butter
1 medium onion, diced
1 lb mushrooms, sliced
1 tomato, chopped

$\frac{1}{2}$ tsp basil
1 tsp parsley
Salt and pepper, to taste
2 to 3 tsp butter (optional)

Heat oil or butter in a large fry pan. Add onion and sauté for 1 minute. Add mushrooms, tomato, basil and parsley and sauté for 3 to 4 minutes, or until almost done. Season to taste and blend in butter, if desired.

Hint: You can spray fry pan with nonstick spray before heating pan and adding oil or butter. If you want, peel and remove seeds from the tomato before adding to the mushrooms.

■ ● ● ● ● ■ ● ● ■ ● ● ■ ● ● ● ● ■ ● ● ■ ● ■ ● ● ■ ● ● ■ ● ■ ● ● ■

Roasted Asparagus

1 lb asparagus
Kosher (or coarse) salt and freshly
  ground black pepper, to taste

1 T olive oil
1 to 2 T lemon juice

Cut thick or woody ends off asparagus and rinse. Spray a baking pan with nonstick spray. Place asparagus in pan and drizzle with olive oil. Sprinkle with salt and pepper. Bake at 500° for 12 to 15 minutes, stirring once or twice, or until al dente. Drizzle with lemon juice, to taste. Serve hot or at room temperature.

Hint: *For added flavor, add 1 to 2 fresh minced garlic cloves before roasting. Asparagus may be left whole or cut into small pieces.*

Roasted Vidalia Onions

2 large Vidalia onions, sliced
2 T olive oil
6 cloves garlic, minced

$\frac{1}{2}$ C fresh mint, chopped
3 T balsamic vinegar
Salt and pepper, to taste

Grease roasting pan or spray pan with nonstick spray. Place everything, except balsamic vinegar, in pan and mix well. Cover pan and bake at 350° for 45 minutes. Remove cover and stir mixture. Bake, uncovered, for 15 additional minutes. Drizzle with balsamic vinegar and adjust seasoning.

Cabbage With Dried Cranberries

6 C (1 medium head) green or Savoy
  cabbage, thinly sliced or shredded
$\frac{1}{2}$ C dried cranberries

1 T butter or margarine
2 to 3 T walnuts, chopped
Salt and pepper, to taste

Steam cabbage and cranberries over a steamer in a large pot until cabbage is crisp-tender, about 5 minutes. Drain and place in a large bowl. Add butter or margarine, nuts and salt and pepper. Toss well.

Cabbage With Pine Nuts

1 medium head green cabbage, coarsely chopped or shredded	2 T lemon juice
2 to 3 T butter or margarine, melted	Salt and pepper, to taste
	$\frac{1}{3}$ C pine nuts, toasted

Bring a large pot of water to a boil and plunge cabbage into it. Allow the water to return to a boil and cook the cabbage for an additional 20 to 30 seconds. Drain and transfer to a heated bowl. Stir in butter or margarine, lemon juice and salt and pepper. Sprinkle with pine nuts.

Sesame Vegetables

1 lb green beans, broccoli, cauliflower or asparagus	2 tsp lemon juice
2 T butter or margarine	2 T sesame seeds, toasted
	Salt and pepper, to taste

Steam or boil vegetables. While vegetables are cooking, melt butter or margarine in a small saucepan over low heat. Add lemon juice and sesame seeds and cook until seeds just begin to brown. Pour over drained vegetables. Add salt and pepper, to taste.

Squash in the Microwave

2 lbs squash such as butternut, acorn, spaghetti or dumpling

Pierce the squash with the tines of a roasting fork in many places. Place on a plate and put in the microwave. Cook, uncovered, on high for 14 to 15 minutes, or until soft, turning over once about halfway through cooking. Remove from microwave and cut squash in half. Allow squash to stand for 2 minutes. Discard seeds. Using a fork, remove squash from the skin, place in a bowl and mash. Season to taste with butter or margarine, brown sugar, cinnamon, salt and pepper, ginger, orange juice or maple syrup.

Hint: *You can use a larger squash but adjust the cooking time. Also, you can use this method to cook pumpkin.*

Microwave Corn on the Cob

Husk corn and rinse. Place in a microwave dish large enough to hold ears of corn. Sprinkle with 2 to 3 tablespoons water. Cover with plastic wrap, piercing with a knife to make a steam vent. Microwave on high for 2 to $2\frac{1}{2}$ minutes per ear.

Hint: *To microwave 5 or 6 ears or corn, place in a 9"x13" glass pan, sprinkle with $\frac{1}{4}$ cup water and cook on high for 12 to 15 minutes, or until tender. This sure beats heating up the kitchen with a large pot of boiling water on top of the stove!*

Hungarian Zucchini

1 T olive or canola oil
1 medium onion, thinly sliced
2 medium-large zucchini, thinly sliced
$\frac{1}{4}$ to $\frac{1}{3}$ C sour cream

1 T fresh dill or 1 tsp dried
1 tsp paprika
Salt, to taste

Heat oil in a large fry pan. Add onion and sauté for 2 to 3 minutes. Add zucchini and sauté for 5 minutes. Add sour cream, dill, paprika and salt and cover the pan. Cook over low-medium heat for about 10 minutes, or until zucchini is tender.

Hint: *You can substitute reduced fat sour cream for regular sour cream.*

Sweet and Sour Zucchini

$1\frac{1}{2}$ tsp olive oil
$1\frac{1}{2}$ tsp butter
1 medium onion, thinly sliced
2 large or 4 small zucchini

$1\frac{1}{2}$ tsp sugar
$\frac{1}{4}$ C chicken or vegetable broth
$1\frac{1}{2}$ to 2 tsp balsamic vinegar
Salt and pepper, to taste

Heat oil in a large fry pan. Add butter. When butter melts, add onion and reduce heat to low and cook the onion for 10 minutes, stirring occasionally. Slice zucchini lengthwise in quarters. Then thinly slice crosswise. When onion is golden, add sugar and cook for 20 to 30 seconds. Add broth and cook for 3 to 4 minutes. Add zucchini. Cover and cook for 10 to 15 minutes, stirring occasionally, until tender. Add balsamic vinegar, salt and pepper.

■ ■

Roasted Garlic

Garlic bulbs   Olive oil

Remove loose outer leaves from garlic bulbs. Cut off tops so that each clove is open at the top. Drizzle about 1 teaspoon olive oil over each bulb. Place bulbs in a garlic baker or covered casserole or wrap bulbs in foil and place on a baking sheet. Roast at 350° for 50 to 60 minutes, or until garlic is tender. Cool until it can be handled. To serve, break apart cloves and squeeze the bottoms so that garlic oozes out the top. Serve with olive oil seasoned with Italian spices or add roasted garlic to mashed potatoes, or sauces, or spread on hot French or Italian bread.

Microwave Method: Cook on high 4 minutes. Allow to cool. For softer consistency, cook a few seconds longer.

Roasted Butternut Squash With Potatoes

2 to 3 T olive oil
3 cloves garlic, minced
1 lb butternut squash, peeled and cut
  into 1" cubes
$\frac{1}{2}$ tsp rosemary

1 lb potatoes, peeled and cut
  into 1" cubes
$\frac{1}{2}$ tsp oregano
Salt and pepper, to taste

Combine oil and garlic in a large roasting pan. Add squash, potatoes, herbs, salt and pepper. Toss well so that the vegetables are all coated with oil. Bake at 400° for 45 minutes, or until veggies are tender and beginning to turn golden.

Hint: *This is especially good with Yukon gold potatoes. To save time, buy fresh peeled and cubed squash from the produce department of your supermarket.*

■ ■

Potato Kugel

3 to 4 T oil
6 medium-large potatoes (2½ lbs)
I large onion
I large carrot

¼ C flour or matzoh meal
I to I½ tsp salt
¼ tsp white pepper
2 eggs, beaten

Place oil in a 9"x13" pan. Place the pan in oven for a few minutes while you prepare the kugel. Scrub potatoes and leave skin on. Peel the carrot. Grate the potatoes, onion and carrot in a food processor. Remove and place in a large bowl. Add remaining ingredients and mix well. When the kugel mixture is ready, remove pan from the oven and pour the hot oil into the potato mixture. Mix and then pour potato mixture into the heated pan. Bake at 375° for I hour, or until golden and crisp at outer edges.

Hint: *Leaving the skin on the potatoes saves time and provides lots of fiber. This recipe can be used during Passover (if using matzoh meal), or throughout the year. Bake and cool completely before freezing. To serve, defrost and heat at 350° until hot.*

Tzimmes With Kishke

2 lbs carrots, peeled and cut
   into I to I½" pieces
2 lbs sweet potatoes, peeled and cut
   into 2" chunks

6 T margarine, cut into small pieces
2 lbs kishke sliced into I" chunks
   (remove skin before cutting)
¾ C maple or pancake syrup

In a large pot, steam carrots and sweet potatoes together until almost tender. Drain and transfer to a greased 4- or 5-quart casserole. Add remaining ingredients and mix well. Bake at 350° for I hour, or until tender. This tastes best if made at least I day in advance.

Hint: *You can use canned or frozen carrots and canned sweet potatoes. Save the juices from the cans and add to the casserole. To use during Passover, substitute ½ cup granulated sugar, ½ cup brown sugar and ½ cup water for the maple or pancake syrup.*

Sweet Potato Cranberry Casserole

4 large sweet potatoes or yams
 (approx. 2½ lbs)
¼ C brown sugar, divided
1 C fresh cranberries, divided

2 T butter or margarine, divided
½ C orange juice
½ C walnuts, chopped
½ tsp cinnamon

Bake sweet potatoes at 400° for approximately 40 to 50 minutes, or in the microwave (see below), until tender. Cool briefly. Remove the skins and mash the potatoes. Place half of the sweet potatoes in a 1½- to 2-quart casserole which has been sprayed with nonstick spray. Sprinkle with half of the brown sugar, ½ cup of the cranberries. Dot with 1 tablespoon butter or margarine. Layer with remaining sweet potatoes, brown sugar, cranberries and butter or margarine. Pour orange juice on top. Cover and bake at 350° for 25 minutes. Sprinkle with walnuts and cinnamon and bake, uncovered, for another 10 to 15 minutes.

Microwave Method: To cook 2 to 2½ pounds sweet potatoes, prick with the tines of a fork, set on a paper towel or plate and cook on high for 8 to 10 minutes, or until tender.

Sweet Potato Casserole

2 lbs sweet potatoes
½ C sugar
1 egg
¼ C raisins
Rind and juice of 1 lemon
¼ tsp nutmeg

¼ C milk
⅓ C pecans, chopped
2 to 3 T butter or margarine
¼ C coconut (optional)
Salt and pepper, to taste

Scrub potatoes and cut an "X" in flesh. Bake at 400° for 40 to 50 minutes, or until tender, or microwave on high by placing the potatoes in a circular pattern on a plate and cooking for about 8 to 10 minutes, or until tender. Cool slightly, remove the skin and mash the potatoes. Add all ingredients and blend well. Pour into a greased 8- or 9-inch casserole and bake at 350° for 30 minutes.

Hint: *If you bake the potatoes in the microwave, this recipe is very quick to prepare. It freezes well. Double the recipe for a 9"x13" pan.*

■ ■

Sweet Potato and Onion Home Fries

4 large sweet potatoes, scrubbed
3 to 4 T butter or margarine
2 medium onions, thinly sliced

$\frac{1}{4}$ tsp nutmeg
Salt and pepper, to taste

Bake sweet potatoes at 400° for 35 to 40 minutes, or until almost tender or microwave on high for about 6 to 8 minutes. Allow to cool and cut into $\frac{1}{4}$-inch slices. Melt the butter or margarine in a large fry pan. Sauté the onions for about 2 to 3 minutes and add precooked sweet potatoes, nutmeg, salt and pepper. Cook on medium heat, stirring frequently, until the potatoes are tender and slightly brown.

Hint: *Leave the skin on the potatoes for added nutrition and flavor.*

Potato and Onion Bake

6 large potatoes, unpeeled
$\frac{1}{4}$ C butter or margarine, melted
3 onions, cut into 1" chunks

$\frac{1}{2}$ tsp garlic powder
$1\frac{1}{2}$ to 2 tsp paprika
Salt and pepper, to taste

Scrub potatoes and cut into halves, lengthwise, then into $\frac{1}{2}$-inch slices crosswise. Melt butter or margarine in a 9"x13" roasting pan and toss potatoes and onions in the pan so that they are evenly coated. Bake at 350° for 1 hour, turning every 15 to 20 minutes. Sprinkle with garlic powder, paprika, salt and pepper and bake for 30 additional minutes, or until potatoes are tender, yet crispy.

Hint: *If you keep paprika refrigerated it will remain potent for much longer than at room temperature.*

Pan-Roasted Dijon Potatoes

6 small red potatoes, quartered
2 cloves garlic, minced
1 tsp butter or margarine, melted

2 to $2\frac{1}{2}$ T Dijon mustard
2 T parsley, finely chopped

Place potatoes and garlic in a heavy fry pan which has been sprayed with a nonstick spray. Cover and cook over low heat for about 35 minutes, stirring occasionally, until tender. Combine butter or margarine, mustard and parsley and toss with cooked potatoes.

■ ■

Red and Orange Roasted Potatoes

$1\frac{1}{2}$ lbs red potatoes, scrubbed and
  cut into 1" cubes
$1\frac{1}{2}$ lbs sweet potatoes, scrubbed and
  cut into 1" cubes

$1\frac{1}{2}$ T olive oil
$1\frac{1}{2}$ tsp rosemary
1 tsp kosher or coarse salt

Spray roasting pan with nonstick cooking spray. Place all ingredients in pan. With a wooden spoon, stir well. Bake at 500° for 20 minutes, stirring occasionally.

Hint: These crispy, delicious potatoes are high in fiber and vitamins and are low in fat.

Roasted Red Potatoes and Green Beans

8 small red potatoes (approx. $1\frac{1}{4}$ lbs),
  unpeeled and cut in quarters
24 whole garlic cloves, peeled
2 to 3 T olive oil, divided

1 lb green beans, ends
  removed and cut in half
$\frac{1}{4}$ C parsley, chopped
Salt and pepper, to taste

Scrub and quarter potatoes. Place in a shallow roasting pan. Add garlic and toss with 1 tablespoon olive oil. Bake at 350° for 35 minutes, stirring once or twice. Toss green beans with 1 tablespoon olive oil and add to potatoes and garlic. Bake for 20 to 25 minutes, stirring 2 or 3 times. Remove from roasting pan and place in a bowl. Toss with parsley, salt and pepper. Add the last tablespoon of oil, if desired. Serve either hot or at room temperature.

Hint: Don't be shocked at the amount of garlic in this recipe. As garlic cooks, it develops a nutty, almost sweet flavor.

■ ■ ■■ ■

Mashed Potatoes

$3\frac{1}{2}$ to 4 lbs potatoes, peeled
  and quartered
1 stick butter or margarine

$\frac{3}{4}$ C hot milk
Salt and white pepper, to taste

Place potatoes in a large saucepan and cover with water. Cover pan and bring to a boil. Reduce heat to low and simmer for approximately 25 minutes, or until potatoes are tender. Drain well. Mash potatoes with a masher, ricer or electric mixer. Add remaining ingredients, to taste.

Variations:

- Very Creamy: Add cream instead of milk and use more butter.
- Onion: Add 1 to 2 chopped onions that have been sautéed in butter or margarine.
- Garlic: Add 1 or 2 heads of garlic that have been roasted, squeezed out of their "paper" and mashed. For more details on roasting garlic, see **Roasted Garlic** (pg. 119).

Hint: *Never use a food processor to mash potatoes because they will end up the consistency of wallpaper paste!*

Hot or Cold New Potatoes

1 lb small new or red potatoes
$\frac{2}{3}$ C sour cream
1 medium onion, finely diced

2 T cilantro or dill, minced
Salt and pepper, to taste

Scrub potatoes, but do not peel. Boil or steam until tender, about 15 minutes. Drain well and slice.

- To serve hot, return potatoes to saucepan and add sour cream, onion, herbs and spices. Heat at low temperature, just until hot.
- To serve cold, remove from saucepan, add remaining ingredients, and serve at room temperature or refrigerate.

Hint: *Low fat sour cream may be substituted for regular sour cream.*

■■■■■■■■■■■■■■■■■■■■■■■■■■■■■

PASTA, RICE AND PIZZA

Oriental Sesame Noodles

1 lb fresh Chinese noodles
3 T sesame seeds, toasted
$\frac{1}{4}$ lb pea pods, broccoli or
   asparagus, blanched
2 scallions, chopped

1 red pepper, cut into thin slices
   about 1" long
2 C cooked shrimp, chicken,
   beef, pork, or tofu (optional)

Dressing:

$\frac{1}{3}$ C sesame oil
3 T rice vinegar
3 T sugar
$\frac{1}{2}$ C soy sauce

$\frac{1}{4}$ C sesame paste (Tahini) or peanut
   butter (freshly ground, preferred)
2 tsp hot (spicy) oil

Combine all ingredients for the dressing and whisk together until well blended. Set aside. To cook noodles, heat 2 quarts of water in a large pot. Break noodles apart into a few handfuls. When the water boils, add noodles. When water comes to a boil again and noodles are al dente, drain and rinse in cool water. Rinse again and drain well. Place in a large bowl. Add the dressing, blanched vegetables, red pepper, sesame seeds and scallions. Add shrimp, chicken, beef, pork or tofu, if desired. Chill for several hours. Remove from the refrigerator about 20 minutes before serving.

Hint: *These noodles make a wonderful vegetarian dish or are delicious with shrimp, cooked chicken beef or pork. You can find sesame oil, rice wine vinegar and hot oil in the Oriental grocery section in most supermarkets. To toast sesame seeds, heat at 350° for 3 minutes, or until they turn a golden color. Watch carefully or they will burn!*

■ ■

Turkish Noodles

1 T olive oil
3 C (6 oz) very fine egg
  noodles, crushed

2 ripe tomatoes, chopped
1⅛ C beef, chicken, or vegetable broth
Salt and pepper, to taste

Heat oil in fry pan. Add noodles and stir on high heat until golden, about 3 to 4 minutes. Add tomatoes, broth, salt and pepper. Lower heat and cook uncovered, stirring occasionally, until broth is completely absorbed, about 10 minutes.

Macaroni and Cottage Cheese Casserole

2 C elbow macaroni
1½ C cottage cheese (fat free or 1%)
¾ C low fat (1%) milk
1 small onion, quartered
1 T flour

1 C reduced fat sharp Cheddar
  cheese, shredded
Salt and pepper, to taste
2 T seasoned bread crumbs
2 T Parmesan or Romano cheese, grated

Cook pasta until al dente and drain. Combine cottage cheese, milk, onion, flour, Cheddar cheese, salt and pepper in a food processor or blender and purée. After the pasta has been drained, put it back in the pot in which it was cooked. Add the cottage cheese mixture and mix well. Pour into a greased 3-quart baking dish. Combine bread crumbs and Parmesan or Romano and sprinkle over the top. Bake at 400° for 28 to 32 minutes, or until golden and bubbly. Allow to sit for at least 5 minutes before serving.

Hint: *This is a very easy and tasty low fat version of a classic dish. If you are cooking for only 1 or 2 people, you can cut the recipe in half and bake it in a smaller dish.*

Orzo With Lemon

2½ C chicken broth
1 C orzo
1 tsp lemon zest, grated

1 tsp olive oil
1½ tsp fresh lemon juice
2 to 3 T parsley or chives, for garnish

Bring the broth to a boil. Add orzo. Reduce heat and simmer, uncovered, just until tender. Drain and return to pan. Add lemon zest, oil and lemon juice. Garnish with parsley or chives, if desired.

Florentine Manicotti

1 medium onion, chopped
2 cloves garlic, minced
1 T olive oil
10 oz pkg frozen chopped spinach,
  cooked and well drained
$\frac{1}{2}$ C Parmesan or Romano
  cheese, grated

1 lb ricotta or cottage cheese
1 egg
Salt and pepper, to taste
10 large manicotti, cooked and drained
20 to 24 oz spaghetti sauce
2 to 3 T grated Parmesan or Romano
  cheese, for sprinkling on top

Sauté onion and garlic in oil until tender. Combine spinach, cheeses, egg, salt and pepper. Add sautéed onion and garlic. Mix well. Using a pastry bag or spoon, fill manicotti with spinach mixture. Place in a greased 9"x13" pan and cover with foil. Bake at 350° for 35 minutes. Heat spaghetti sauce. Remove foil and pour sauce over manicotti. Sprinkle with additional Parmesan or Romano cheese and bake, uncovered, for 10 more minutes.

Hint: *Low fat or fat free ricotta or cottage cheese can be used in this recipe.*

Risotto a la Milanese

3 T butter, divided
1 medium onion, finely chopped
2 C raw long grain rice
$\frac{1}{4}$ C dry white wine

$4\frac{1}{2}$ C boiling chicken broth
2 T parsley, finely minced
$\frac{1}{2}$ C Parmesan cheese, grated
Salt, to taste

In a 2- or 3-quart saucepan, heat chicken broth until it boils. Continue boiling until it is all used in the recipe. In another saucepan, melt 2 tablespoons of the butter. Add onions and cook until onions soften. Stir in the rice, and cook until it is yellow or almost golden. Add the wine and cook until it is absorbed. Add 1 cup of the boiling broth. Cover pan and cook until it is absorbed. Repeat 3 more times, (adding 1 cup at a time) until all broth has been absorbed and rice is al dente. The total cooking time is about 30 minutes. Stir in remaining tablespoon of butter, parsley and cheese. Remove from heat and let stand, covered, for 5 minutes before serving. Season with salt, to taste.

Microwave Wild Mushroom Risotto

2 scallions, sliced
2 cloves garlic, minced
$\frac{1}{2}$ onion, chopped
$2\frac{3}{4}$ C chicken or vegetable broth
1 C arborio rice

2 T Parmesan cheese
6 oz wild mushrooms (shitake,
  portobello), sliced
Salt and pepper, to taste

Combine scallions, onion and garlic in a large microwaveable bowl and cook on high for 4 minutes. Add broth and rice. Cover and microwave on high for 15 minutes. Stir in mushrooms and cover and cook on high for 8 minutes. Stir in Parmesan. Season with salt and pepper. To make half the amount, cook on medium.

Hint: If you don't have wild mushrooms you can use regular button mushrooms. Another option is to use dried wild mushrooms such as shitake or porcinis. However, if you use dried mushrooms, soak them in warm water until they are soft and use the liquid they were softened in, strained, as part of the broth.

Sun Dried Tomato Risotto

10 sun dried tomatoes
1 C water
$2\frac{1}{2}$ C chicken or vegetable broth
2 T olive oil
1 large onion, finely chopped

2 cloves garlic, minced
1 C arborio rice
$\frac{1}{3}$ C Parmesan cheese, grated
Salt and pepper, to taste
Chopped parsley, for garnish (optional)

In a small saucepan, simmer the tomatoes in water for about 1 minute. Drain and reserve liquid. Chop tomatoes. In a medium saucepan, combine reserved cooking liquid and broth and bring to a simmer. Regulate heat to keep liquid simmering. In a large saucepan, heat the olive oil and add the onion and garlic and stir until softened. Add the rice and stir until the grains are all coated with oil. Add chopped tomatoes and $\frac{1}{2}$ cup of the simmering liquid. Cook over medium heat, stirring until liquid has been absorbed. Continue adding the liquid, $\frac{1}{2}$ cup at a time, until it is all absorbed, approximately 18 minutes. Stir in the Parmesan, salt and pepper. Sprinkle with parsley, if desired.

Hint: You can cut the sun dried tomatoes with a scissors before soaking them and then you won't have to chop them later. Also, you can pour 1 cup of boiling water over the tomatoes and let them sit for a minute, rather than cooking them on the stove.

■ ■

Red and Green Pepper Sauce for Pasta

1 T olive oil
2 medium onions, chopped
1 large red pepper, chopped
1 large green pepper, chopped

Salt and pepper, to taste
$\frac{3}{4}$ C all-purpose cream
$\frac{3}{4}$ to 1 lb spaghetti or linguine,
   cooked and drained

Heat oil in a skillet and add onions. Sauté until onions are soft, but not brown. Add peppers and cook until tender. Add cream and turn heat to medium-high. Cook just until cream is reduced by half. Serve over hot pasta.

Hint: *This sauce is wonderful when you want a "quick fix" for something rich and delicious.*

Apple Rice Pilaf

1 to 2 T olive oil or butter or margarine
1 medium onion, chopped
1 stalk celery, chopped
Rind of 1 orange, grated
1 C white or brown rice

$\frac{1}{4}$ C parsley, minced, divided
2 C apple cider or apple juice
$\frac{1}{2}$ C dried cranberries or raisins
Salt and pepper, to taste

Heat oil, butter or margarine in a saucepan. Add onion, celery and orange rind and sauté until vegetables are limp. Add rice and continue cooking just until rice is golden. Add half the parsley, cider or apple juice and dried cranberries or raisins. Bring to a boil. Cover and reduce heat to a simmer. Cook for 25 minutes for white rice and almost an hour for brown rice. Add salt and pepper, to taste. Sprinkle remaining parsley on top just before serving.

Hint: *This pilaf has a fruity taste and goes especially well with poultry, pork or lamb.*

Brown Rice Pilaf With Pine Nuts and Raisins

$\frac{1}{2}$ C golden raisins or combination
  of golden and dark raisins
$\frac{1}{4}$ C dry sherry
I to 2 T olive oil
I medium onion, chopped

$\frac{1}{2}$ C pine nuts or slivered almonds
$1\frac{1}{2}$ C brown rice
$3\frac{1}{2}$ C chicken or vegetable broth
Salt and pepper, to taste
2 T fresh parsley, minced

Soak raisins in sherry for at least 15 minutes. Heat oil in a heavy pan. Stir in onion and cook until soft. Stir in pine nuts and cook until they take on a little color. Add rice and stir until it becomes a golden color. Add broth and sherry-soaked raisins and bring to a boil. Turn heat down to a simmer and cover casserole. Cook for 50 to 60 minutes without removing cover. Then remove cover and fluff rice with a fork to ensure that all the liquid has been absorbed and that rice is tender. Add salt and pepper, to taste. If not tender, cover and cook for an additional 5 to 10 minutes. Sprinkle with minced parsley.

Hint: *Brown rice has a slightly nutty flavor and chewier texture than white rice. It is also healthier than white rice because it contains more fiber, protein and vitamin E.*

Couscous With Raisins and Pine Nuts

2 C chicken or vegetable broth
2 T raisins
I T olive oil
I C couscous

2 T chives, chopped
2 T pine nuts, toasted
Rind of I lemon, grated
Salt and pepper, to taste

In medium saucepan, combine broth, raisins and olive oil. Bring to a boil. Remove from heat and stir in couscous, chives, pine nuts and lemon rind. Cover and let stand for 5 minutes. Fluff with a fork.

Hint: *Couscous is very tiny pasta that cooks just by being mixed with the boiling broth. The raisins, lemon rind and nuts yield an interesting combination of both texture and flavor. You can substitute slivered almonds for the pine nuts.*

■ ■

Oriental Linguine With Pea Pods

8 oz linguine	2 tsp sugar
4 T soy sauce	1 tsp fresh ginger, grated
2 T sesame oil	2 tsp canola or peanut oil
2 T rice vinegar	$\frac{1}{3}$ lb pea pods, cut in thirds at an angle

Boil linguine in a large pot of water. Drain well. Combine all other ingredients, except pea pods and oil, in a jar and shake until well blended. Add this mixture to the linguine and toss. Heat oil in a fry pan or wok and stir-fry the pea pods briefly, just until they are bright green and lightly browned. Add to the linguine. Chill for a few hours or overnight. Serve cold or at room temperature.

Hint: *You can use less pea pods and substitute sliced mushrooms, sliced water chestnuts and/or sliced red peppers. If you want to omit the step of stir-frying the pea pods, just blanch them in boiling water for about 30 to 45 seconds, or until they turn bright green. Immediately plunge them into cold water until cooled down and drain.*

Spaghetti With Artichokes

$13\frac{3}{4}$ oz can artichokes packed in water or 1 box frozen artichoke hearts, defrosted and drained	3 to 4 cloves garlic, minced
	$\frac{1}{4}$ C parsley, minced
$\frac{1}{2}$ C bread crumbs	$\frac{1}{4}$ to $\frac{1}{3}$ C olive oil
$\frac{1}{2}$ C Romano cheese, grated	$\frac{1}{2}$ lb spaghetti

Cut artichokes into small pieces. Combine with other ingredients, except spaghetti. Place in a greased roasting pan. Bake at 350° for 20 to 25 minutes, stirring occasionally. Meanwhile cook spaghetti in a large pot of boiling water. When al dente, drain and add to roasted artichoke mixture. Mix well and bake for an additional 10 minutes.

Hint: *If you really love artichokes, add another can. This is my oldest son's favorite.*

Spinach Pesto Over Linguine

1 lb linguine, cooked and drained
10 oz pkg frozen spinach, thawed
  and well drained
2 T olive oil
$\frac{1}{4}$ C Parmesan cheese, grated
2 T parsley, chopped
2 cloves garlic

$\frac{1}{2}$ tsp basil
2 T butter
$\frac{1}{3}$ C boiling water
4 to 6 oz Feta cheese
Salt and pepper, to taste
Fresh tomato chunks, for garnish

While linguine is cooking, make the pesto sauce. In a food processor or blender, combine the spinach, oil, Parmesan cheese, parsley, garlic and basil. Process or blend until finely chopped. Melt butter in the boiling water. With the processor or blender running, pour the melted butter mixture into the sauce until well blended. Pour the sauce over the pasta and toss until the pasta is coated. Add Feta cheese and season with salt and pepper. Garnish with tomato chunks, if desired.

Hint: You can substitute other shapes of pasta for the linguine. This pesto is a lot lower in fat than traditional pesto sauce.

Tortellini Primavera

$2\frac{1}{2}$ C vegetables, diced (use any
  combination of carrots, zucchini,
  broccoli, yellow squash, red, green
  or yellow peppers or tomatoes)
1 lb cheese tortellini

3 to 4 T olive oil, or to taste
$\frac{1}{2}$ to $\frac{3}{4}$ C Parmesan cheese, grated
$\frac{1}{4}$ C parsley, minced
Salt and pepper, to taste

Blanch all veggies, except pepper and tomatoes, just until brightly colored and still crisp. Plunge into cold water and drain. Cook the tortellini in a large pot of boiling salted water until they rise to the top and are al dente. Drain and toss with olive oil until well coated. Add vegetables, Parmesan cheese, parsley, salt and pepper. Serve immediately or refrigerate and bring to room temperature before serving.

Hint: This is especially delicious in the summer when local produce is at its peak.

Sun Dried Tomato Pesto Butter

$\frac{1}{3}$ C sun dried tomatoes, drained
  if packed in oil, <u>or</u> if using
  dried tomatoes, soak in
  water until soft, and drain

$\frac{1}{4}$ C Parmesan cheese
1 large clove garlic
$\frac{1}{2}$ C butter, softened
Salt and pepper, to taste

Place tomatoes, Parmesan cheese and garlic in food processor. Using the steel blade of the processor, mix until finely chopped. Add butter, salt and pepper and mix well. Transfer to covered jars or crocks and refrigerate until serving. Use as a spread on toasted Italian or French bread or on hot pasta or rice. You can also melt this, and drizzle it on fish before cooking.

Hint: To make **Parsley Pesto Butter**, substitute $\frac{3}{4}$ cup lightly packed fresh parsley for the sun dried tomatoes. To give as a gift, put pesto butter in decorative jars or crocks.

Pesto and Ricotta Calzone

$\frac{1}{2}$ C pesto sauce
$\frac{3}{4}$ C ricotta cheese
1 egg, beaten

$\frac{1}{4}$ C Parmesan cheese, grated
2 to 3 tsp olive oil (optional)
Pizza crust or 1 lb pizza dough

Combine all ingredients except oil. Spread over one-half of a 12-inch whole wheat or white pizza crust. Fold the other half of dough over like a turnover, and pinch to seal. Bake at 500° for 8 to 10 minutes on the lowest rack of the oven. Remove from oven and brush with olive oil, if desired. Allow to cool for 2 minutes before slicing.

Hint: Use homemade or prepared pesto sauce. Use homemade **Pizza** (pg. 134) dough or buy the dough from a bakery.

Pizza

Featured in Cover Photo

Dough:

5 C flour

1 tsp salt

2 T sugar

2 pkgs yeast

$1\frac{3}{4}$ to 2 C warm water (105° to 115°)

Combine flour, salt, sugar and yeast in a large bowl. Add 1 cup of the warm water. Add $\frac{1}{4}$ cup of water at a time from the remaining cup, until all flour is absorbed and a firm dough is attained. Depending on the weather, the amount of water added may change. Turn onto a lightly floured surface and let rise for 10 minutes. Knead for 3 to 4 minutes or mix in an electric mixer equipped with a dough hook. Place in a large, lightly greased bowl, turning to grease the top. Cover with a clean towel and set aside to rise until doubled in size, about 1 hour. Punch dough down. Knead again on a lightly floured surface for about 3 to 4 minutes. Form into a ball and divide exactly into thirds (if using 12-inch pans) or into halves (if using 16-inch pans) with serrated edge knife. Cover and let rise until doubled or use refrigerator method (instead of letting dough rise a second time, place it in a covered bowl in the refrigerator and let it rise slowly until doubled). Dough will be ready once it has doubled and will hold for up to 24 hours at this point or can be frozen. On a lightly floured surface, roll and stretch into a circle large enough to fit pizza pan. Oil the pans and sprinkle with a little corn meal before placing dough on them.

Yield: (2) 16-inch or (3) 12-inch pizza crusts

Whole Wheat Dough:

1 C warm water (105° to 115°)

1 pkg yeast (1 scant tablespoon)

1 tsp sugar

$1\frac{1}{2}$ C whole wheat flour

1 T canola or olive oil

$\frac{1}{2}$ tsp salt

1 to $1\frac{1}{2}$ C all-purpose flour

Place water in a large bowl. Add the yeast and sugar and mix until dissolved. Let mixture stand 5 to 15 minutes, or until bubbly. Add the whole wheat flour, oil, salt and 1 cup or more of the all-purpose flour, as needed, to form a ball of dough that pulls away from the sides of the bowl. Turn the dough onto a floured surface and knead for about 5 minutes, adding more all-purpose flour, as needed, to make a firm dough that is not sticky. Place dough in a greased bowl, turning to grease the top. Cover with plastic wrap or a towel and set aside in a warm, draft-free place, to rise until it has doubled in bulk. At this point, dough can be placed in the refrigerator for several hours and allowed to rise there. Remove from the refrigerator about 30 minutes before rolling out.

Yield: (1) 12- to 16-inch pizza crust

***Hint**: You can freeze the dough for later use. Defrost completely before rolling out.*

■■■■■■■■■■ ■■■■■■■■■■■■■■■■■■■■

Pizza (continued)

Sauce:

6 oz can tomato paste
1 to 2 tsp Italian seasoning

12 oz can ground or crushed
Italian tomatoes

Whisk ingredients together and spread over dough.

Cheese:

1 lb Mozzarella cheese, shredded
5 oz Romano or Parmesan cheese

2 to 3 tsp olive oil (optional)

Sprinkle one-third to one-half of the Mozzarella (depending on whether you are making 2 or 3 pizzas) over the sauce. Scatter one-third to one-half of the Romano or Parmesan between the spaces of the Mozzarella. If desired, drizzle olive oil over cheese.

Variations or Additional Toppings:

- Peppers: For crisp peppers, place thinly sliced peppers on top of pizza; for softer peppers, sauté peppers in oil before placing on pizza or cook them in the microwave for 1 minute.
- Pepperoni: Slice thinly and place pepperoni on top of most of the cheese. Then cover pepperoni with remaining cheese.
- Hamburger: Brown hamburger and sprinkle over pizza.
- Onion: Chop or slice thinly and sprinkle over pizza.
- Mushrooms: Thinly slice and place on top of pizza.
- Sausage: Remove Italian sausage from its casing and break into small pieces. Brown in a fry pan, drain and sprinkle over pizza.
- Meatball: Slice cold meatballs and place on top of pizza.
- Combination: Use any or all of the above.

To bake, set your oven as high as it will go (approximately 550°), well in advance. Bake 1 pizza at a time on the lowest shelf in the oven. When the top crust starts to get golden around the edges, fold up a piece of the bottom with a knife and look for patches of golden brown and feel for stiffness. This usually takes 8 to 10 minutes. The deeper the patches, the crispier the crust.

Hint: *Have fun, experiment with different cheeses and toppings!*

■ ■

Grilled Pizza

Use **Pizza** (see pg. 134) dough recipe and divide it into 4 sections. Heat the grill to medium-high. Oil an unrimmed cookie sheet or pizza pan and roll out or stretch dough until it is about 8 inches in diameter and quite thin. It doesn't have to be a perfect circle. Holding the cookie sheet near the grill, gently slide the dough onto the hot grill. Cook until the dough puffs slightly, the underside stiffens, and grill marks appear on the bottom of the dough. Using tongs or a wide spatula, flip the pizza back over and onto the cookie sheet so that the grilled side is facing up. Top pizza, as desired. Return the pizza to the grill, with uncooked side facing down. Close the grill or cover the pizza with a pot lid or loosely tented foil. Grill until cheeses melt and dough is cooked through and lightly browned.

Yield: 4 grilled pizzas

Hint: *You need to watch the grill carefully to regulate the heat so that it is hot enough to cook, but not too hot that the dough will burn. Use your imagination to make whatever combination of veggies, herbs, cheese, etc. that you like. It's fun to have each family member or guest choose their own toppings and make their own "personal pizza."*

Garlic Pizza

2 whole bulbs garlic
1 to 1½ T olive oil

1½ C Mozzarella cheese, shredded
¼ C Parmesan cheese, grated

Roast garlic (see **Roasted Garlic** on pg. 119) or steam unpeeled whole garlic bulbs in a vegetable steamer for approximately 15 minutes, or until soft. Let cool until you can handle them. Peel. Using a fork, mash garlic into a paste. Spread over a 12-inch unbaked pizza crust. Drizzle with oil and sprinkle with both cheeses. Bake on the lowest rack of the oven at 550° for 8 to 10 minutes, or until golden.

Hint: *You can substitute Provolone, Fontina or Port Salut for Mozzarella cheese. Substitute Romano or Asiago for Parmesan.*

VEGETARIAN

For additional vegetarian recipes, consult the index under "vegetarian."

Escarole With Beans

1 T olive oil
3 cloves garlic, minced
1 large bunch escarole (about $1\frac{1}{2}$ lbs), coarsely chopped

15 oz can cannellini beans, undrained
1 C chicken or vegetable broth
Salt and pepper, to taste
Parmesan cheese (optional)

Heat oil in a large pot until hot. Add garlic and cook for 1 minute. Add escarole, beans and broth. Season with salt and pepper. Cover and cook for 3 minutes, or until escarole is wilted. Uncover and cook for 10 additional minutes. Ladle into bowls and sprinkle with Parmesan cheese, if desired. Serve with crusty Italian bread.

Hint: *You can use low sodium broth, if desired. This is very high in fiber.*

Speedy Vegetarian Chili

$\frac{3}{4}$ C ($1\frac{1}{2}$ oz) sun dried tomatoes
28 to 30 oz spaghetti sauce
(2) 15 to 16 oz cans kidney beans, rinsed and drained
2 to 3 tsp chili powder

2 to 3 tsp cumin
$\frac{1}{8}$ to $\frac{1}{4}$ tsp cayenne pepper
Salt, to taste
Cheddar cheese, shredded (optional)

Using kitchen shears, snip dried tomatoes into small pieces. Combine all ingredients in a saucepan and bring to a boil. Reduce heat and simmer for 12 minutes, stirring occasionally. Top with Cheddar cheese. Serve with rice, pasta or corn bread.

Hint: *Adjust the seasonings to your own taste buds.*

Vegetarian Chili

1 medium onion, chopped	$15\frac{1}{2}$ oz can chickpeas (garbanzo beans)
$1\frac{1}{4}$ C green peppers, diced	$15\frac{1}{2}$ oz can black beans
$1\frac{1}{4}$ C red peppers, diced	2 C corn (canned or frozen)
2 cloves garlic, minced	2 T tomato paste
$1\frac{1}{2}$ to 2 T chili powder, or to taste	1 T balsamic vinegar
2 tsp sugar	Salt and pepper, to taste
28 oz can crushed tomatoes	Few T shredded Cheddar or Monterey
$15\frac{1}{2}$ oz can kidney beans	Jack cheese (optional)

Rinse and drain all the beans. Spray a heated soup pot with nonstick spray. Add onion, peppers, and garlic and sauté until tender. Add remaining ingredients. Heat until it comes to a boil. Cover and reduce to a simmer. Cook for 1 hour. Serve with brown rice, corn bread or tortilla chips. If you like, garnish each serving with cheese.

Hint: *This recipe is extremely high in fiber and very low in fat.*

Quesadillas With Peppers and Onions

3 to 4 tsp olive oil, divided	1 tsp cumin
1 large onion, thinly sliced	8 oz Cheddar, Monterey Jack or
2 large red, green, orange or yellow	Mexican blend cheese, shredded
peppers, or combination,	(8) 6" flour tortillas
thinly sliced	Salsa, for garnish

Heat 1 to 2 tablespoons of olive oil in a large skillet. Sauté onion and peppers until they begin to soften and onion starts looking translucent. Stir in cumin and remove from pan. Place tortillas on 2 cookie sheets. Sprinkle $\frac{1}{4}$ cup cheese on each tortilla and cover half with one-eighth of the onion and pepper mixture. Fold tortillas in half. Brush lightly with remaining olive oil. Bake at 425° for 7 to 9 minutes, or until cheese is melted and tortillas are lightly browned. Serve with salsa, if desired.

Yield: 8 quesadillas

Hint: *For added taste and color, try using flavored tortillas such as spinach, herb or tomato.*

Sweet Potato Quesadillas

2 T canola or olive oil
2 medium onions, diced
3 cloves garlic, minced
4 C sweet potato or yams,
  peeled and grated
$\frac{3}{4}$ tsp oregano
1 tsp chili powder

$2\frac{1}{2}$ tsp cumin
Pinch cayenne pepper, or to taste
Salt and pepper, to taste
1 C sharp Cheddar cheese, grated
(8) 8" to 10" tortillas
Salsa, for garnish

Heat oil in fry pan and sauté onions and garlic until onions are translucent. Add sweet potatoes, oregano, chili powder, cumin and cayenne. Cook, covered, for about 10 minutes, stirring often. When potato is tender, add salt and pepper and more cayenne, if desired. Cool mixture for a few minutes. Heat tortillas in a lightly oiled fry pan. Spread one-eighth of filling onto half of each tortilla. Sprinkle with 2 tablespoons of cheese. Fold plain half of tortilla over the filling and cook on each side for about 2 to 3 minutes, or until filling is hot and cheese begins to melt. Garnish with salsa.

Yield: 8 quesadillas

Hint: *Keep quesadillas warm in a 250⁰ oven until ready to serve.*

Bulgur Pilaf With Apples and Nuts

1 T olive oil
1 small onion, chopped
1 C bulgur wheat
$\frac{1}{2}$ C raisins
1 C apple cider or apple juice

2 C vegetable broth
1 apple, chopped
$\frac{1}{3}$ C pecans or walnuts, chopped
Salt and pepper, to taste

Heat oil in a large sauce pan. Add onion and sauté for about 2 minutes. Add bulgur, raisins, cider or juice and broth. Bring to a boil, reduce heat and cover. Simmer for 10 minutes. Add apple and nuts and simmer, covered, for about 5 additional minutes, or until liquid has been absorbed.

■ ■

Spinach and Cheese Enchiladas

10 oz bag fresh spinach or
  10 oz frozen spinach,
  defrosted and well drained
2 tsp olive oil
4 cloves garlic, minced
1 lb ricotta cheese

4 oz Cheddar or Monterey Jack
  cheese, shredded
1 T cumin
Salt and pepper, to taste
10 flour tortillas
12 to 16 oz salsa

If using fresh spinach, remove stems and wash and chop the leaves. Heat oil in a large skillet. Add garlic and cook for 1 minute. Add spinach, cover and cook until wilted. Turn off heat and stir in shredded cheese, ricotta and cumin. Spoon spinach mixture evenly onto 8 tortillas. Roll up and place in a greased 9"x13" pan. Pour salsa on top and bake, covered, at 375° for 15 to 20 minutes, or until hot.

Pad Thai

6 to 8 oz thin rice stick noodles
$\frac{1}{4}$ C rice vinegar
$\frac{1}{4}$ C bottled Thai fish sauce
1 T sesame oil
$\frac{1}{4}$ C sugar
1 tsp chili powder
1 to 2 tsp canola or peanut oil

3 cloves garlic, minced
2 eggs, beaten
4 scallions, chopped
$\frac{1}{4}$ lb bean sprouts
$\frac{1}{2}$ lb firm tofu, cut into $\frac{1}{4}$" cubes (optional)
2 to 3 T cilantro, chopped
$\frac{1}{2}$ to $\frac{3}{4}$ C peanuts, finely chopped

Soak noodles in warm water for 20 minutes. Drain. In a small bowl, combine rice vinegar, fish sauce, sesame oil, sugar and chili powder. In a wok or large fry pan, heat the canola or peanut oil and cook garlic for about 1 minute. Pour the eggs into the pan and whisk until they are scrambled. Add the soaked noodles and stir for 1 minute. Add reserved vinegar mixture and bean sprouts. Add tofu, if desired. Stir constantly for 1 more minute. Transfer to a serving dish or platter and sprinkle with cilantro and peanuts.

Hint: *Fish sauce is one of the most common ingredients in Thai cooking. It is made from anchovy extract and sea salt. If you want to add shrimp, pork, beef or tofu, cook it with the garlic and then add the remaining ingredients.*

Bean Burgers

1 medium onion, chopped
2 cloves garlic, minced
2 T olive oil, divided
15 to 19 oz can cannellini
  (white kidney) beans,
  rinsed and drained

1 egg
$\frac{1}{3}$ C bread crumbs
2 T parsley
1 tsp cumin
$\frac{1}{2}$ tsp chili powder
Salt and black pepper, to taste

Sauté onion and garlic in 1 tablespoon of the olive oil until soft. Drain and rinse beans. Place beans, egg, bread crumbs, parsley and seasoning in a food processor or blender and purée. Add sautéed onion and garlic mixture and blend well. Cool slightly. Heat remaining tablespoon oil in fry pan. Using a large spoon, drop bean mixture into pan to make 6 or 7 patties, flattening each with the back of the spoon. Fry on 1 side until golden. Turn over and fry until second side is golden. Serve with vegetables and salad or stuff into pita bread with lettuce and tomato.

Hint: *You can use an egg substitute instead of an egg if you want to lower the fat and cholesterol. There burgers taste very similar to falafel, Middleastern patties made of ground chickpeas.*

Skinny Sloppy Joes

$\frac{1}{2}$ C (1 small) onion, chopped
$\frac{1}{2}$ C (1 stalk) celery, chopped
$\frac{1}{2}$ C (1 medium) carrot, diced
$\frac{1}{2}$ C ($\frac{1}{2}$ pepper) green or
  red pepper, diced
1 clove garlic, minced
$14\frac{1}{2}$ oz can whole tomatoes, undrained

1 to $1\frac{1}{2}$ T chili powder, or to taste
1 T tomato paste
1 T vinegar
Black pepper, to taste
15 to 19 oz can kidney beans,
  rinsed and drained
6 bulkie rolls

Coat a large pan with nonstick spray and place over medium-high heat until hot. Add onion, celery, carrot, pepper and garlic and sauté until tender. Add tomatoes which have been chopped or mashed with a potato masher, chili powder, tomato paste, vinegar and black pepper. Cover and simmer for 10 minutes. Add the kidney beans and cook for 5 additional minutes, or until hot. Cut the rolls in half and place on individual serving plates. Spoon sloppy joe mixture over rolls. This can also be served over rice or pasta instead of rolls.

Hint: *This recipe is nearly fat free.*

Pasta Fagiole in the Crock Pot

1 large onion, chopped
5 to 6 cloves garlic, minced
1 T olive oil
28 oz can peeled tomatoes
2 T parsley, chopped
30 oz chicken or vegetable broth

1 C elbow macaroni, cooked and drained
19 oz can cannellini (white
   kidney) beans, drained
Salt and pepper, to taste
Freshly grated Parmesan or Romano
   cheese, to taste

Sauté the onion and garlic in oil until soft. Chop the tomatoes or mash with a potato masher and place in crock pot. Add sautéed onion and garlic. Add parsley and broth. Cook in a crock pot on low for 3 hours or on high for 2 hours. While tomato mixture is cooking, cook and drain macaroni and drain cannellini beans. Add pasta and beans to the crock pot at the end of cooking time. Cook for a few more minutes, just until everything is hot. Add more salt, pepper and parsley, if desired. Garnish with grated cheese.

Bean and Chili Spread

1 to 2 tsp olive or canola oil
1 medium onion, chopped
3 garlic cloves, minced
(2) 16 oz cans kidney beans,
   drained and rinsed

4 oz can green chilies,
   drained and chopped
12 oz salsa
1 tsp coriander

Heat oil in a small skillet and sauté onion and garlic until tender. In a food processor, using the steel blade, or in a blender, purée the beans and chilies. Add cooked onion and garlic and remaining ingredients. Purée until smooth. Serve with pita bread or veggies or as a filling for quesadillas.

Hint: *The spiciness of this dip varies according to the spiciness of the salsa.*

PASSOVER

Passover Rolls

1 C water	1 C matzoh meal
$\frac{1}{3}$ C peanut or canola oil	4 eggs
Salt, to taste	

In a large saucepan, boil water with oil and salt over medium heat. When water boils, turn heat off and add matzoh meal. Stir until it leaves the sides of the pan. Remove from heat and cool slightly. Add 1 egg at a time, mixing with a wooden spoon. Place tablespoonfuls of batter onto a greased cookie sheet. Bake at 450° for 15 to 20 minutes, reduce heat to 325° and bake for an additional 15 to 20 minutes, or until golden.

Yield: 12 rolls

Hint: These "rolls" are what get the family through "brown bag" lunches during Passover. They can be filled with anything that one would usually put in a sandwich.

Passover Blueberry Muffins

$\frac{1}{2}$ C butter or margarine	$\frac{1}{2}$ C cake meal
$\frac{3}{4}$ C sugar	$\frac{1}{2}$ tsp salt
3 eggs	1 C fresh or frozen blueberries

Cream together butter or margarine and sugar. Add eggs, cake meal and salt. Fold in blueberries by hand. Place in paper-lined cupcake pans and bake at 350° for 45 minutes to 1 hour, or until a toothpick, inserted in the center, comes out clean.

Yield: 12 muffins

Hint: Chopped cranberries and or apples may be substituted for the blueberries. Frozen cranberries can be chopped in a food processor using the steel blade. A combination of cranberries and apples is very tasty.

■ ■

Potato and Mushroom Passover Knishes

Dough:

2 C potatoes (4 medium-large)
2 eggs
1 T potato starch

$\frac{1}{4}$ C matzoh meal
$\frac{1}{4}$ tsp white pepper

Filling:

1 C onions, chopped
$\frac{1}{4}$ C mushrooms
$\frac{1}{4}$ tsp white pepper

Salt, to taste
2 T margarine, melted

Cook potatoes until tender. While potatoes are cooking, sauté the onions, mushrooms and seasonings for the filling. Drain and mash potatoes and add remaining ingredients for dough. Shape dough into 2-inch balls, reserving about one-quarter of the dough. Scoop out a hole in the center of each "knish" ball and place a small amount of the filling into it. Cover with reserved dough and brush with melted margarine. Bake at 375° for 20 to 25 minutes, or until golden.

Hint: *You can substitute ground cooked and seasoned beef for the potato.*

Matzanya

2 C spaghetti sauce
Oregano and basil, to taste
Onions or green peppers, diced
  and sautéed to add to spaghetti
  sauce (optional)

1 egg, beaten
1 lb ricotta cheese
8 oz Mozzarella cheese
3 matzoh

Season spaghetti sauce with dried herbs and sautéed vegetables. Combine egg, ricotta cheese and half the Mozzarella cheese. Slightly dampen matzoh under running water to soften. Grease an 8- or 9-inch square pan. Pour in 1 cup of the spaghetti sauce. Place a piece of matzoh on top to cover. Spread with half of the cheese mixture. Add another piece of matzoh, remaining cheese mixture and top with third piece of matzoh. Pour on remaining spaghetti sauce. Sprinkle with remaining half of Mozzarella. Bake at 350° for 35 minutes, or until set. Allow to cool for 10 minutes before cutting.

Hint: *To double, bake in a 9"x13" pan and increase baking time accordingly.*

■■■■■■■■■■ ■■■■■■■■■■■■■■

Chicken Breasts With Passover Stuffing and Cumberland Sauce

4 T margarine
$\frac{1}{2}$ to $\frac{3}{4}$ lb mushrooms, chopped
4 stalks celery, diced
2 large onions, diced
1 large carrot, grated ($\frac{3}{4}$ C)
$1\frac{1}{2}$ C matzoh meal
1 egg

$\frac{3}{4}$ to 1 C chicken broth
Salt and pepper, to taste
14 to 15 boneless chicken breast halves
1 C currant jelly
$\frac{1}{4}$ C Dijon mustard
$\frac{1}{3}$ C currants (optional)

Melt margarine in a large fry pan. Add mushrooms, celery and onions and sauté until soft, but not brown. Add carrot. Transfer veggies to a bowl and add matzoh meal, egg and enough broth to keep the mixture fairly loose. Season to taste. Using a pounder, flatten chicken breasts. Place a mound of stuffing in the widest end of each breast half and roll up. Place all the stuffed breasts, seam-side down, in a greased baking pan. Make **Cumberland Sauce** by heating currant jelly and mustard in a sauce pan, whisking until melted and smooth. Add currants, if desired. Pour over the chicken. Cover the pan with foil and bake at 350° for 25 to 30 minutes. Remove foil and baste chicken with the juices in the pan. Bake for about 15 to 25 minutes more, basting occasionally, until chicken is completely cooked. If you want to brown the chicken, broil it for about 5 minutes.

Hint: *You can easily cut this recipe in half if you only want to make 7 or 8 stuffed breasts.* **Cumberland Sauce** *can also be used for other chicken recipes.*

Easy Eggplant Creole

1 small eggplant, peeled and cubed
1 medium green pepper, chopped
1 large onion, chopped

$10\frac{1}{2}$ oz can tomato and mushroom sauce
  or spaghetti sauce
Salt and pepper, to taste

Put all ingredients into a saucepan and bring to a boil. Reduce heat to low and cook for 30 minutes, or until vegetables are tender, stirring occasionally.

Hint: *This is a quick and healthy way to cook eggplant.*

■ ■

Matzoh Balls

2 T chicken fat or oil
2 eggs, slightly beaten
$\frac{1}{2}$ C matzoh meal

$\frac{1}{2}$ tsp salt
2 T soup stock or water

Combine chicken fat or oil and eggs. Combine matzoh meal and salt and add to egg mixture. When well blended, add soup stock or water and mix well. Cover mixing bowl and place in the refrigerator for at least 40 minutes. Using a 2- or 3-quart pot, bring salted water to a brisk boil. Reduce heat and into the slightly bubbling water drop balls formed from the above mixture. Cover pot and cook for 30 to 40 minutes. Remove the matzoh balls from the water and drain. You can make the matzoh balls a couple of days ahead and store them in a covered container in the refrigerator. When ready to serve, place them in hot chicken soup and heat until the matzoh balls are hot.

Yield: 8 matzoh balls

Hint: *These are my family's favorite matzoh balls so I always make a quadruple batch. They can be frozen. Defrost before adding to warm soup. Heat until soup and matzoh balls are hot.*

Apple Matzoh Kugel

4 matzoh
3 eggs, well beaten
$\frac{1}{2}$ tsp salt
$\frac{1}{2}$ C sugar
$\frac{1}{4}$ C margarine, melted
I tsp cinnamon

$\frac{1}{2}$ C walnuts, chopped
2 large apples, peeled and chopped
$\frac{1}{2}$ C raisins
$1\frac{1}{2}$ T margarine, cut into cubes,
    for topping

Break matzoh into pieces and soak in water until soft. Drain, but don't squeeze. Beat eggs with salt, sugar, margarine and cinnamon. Add to matzoh. Stir in nuts, apples and raisins. Pour into a greased 9-inch square pan. Dot with margarine cubes. Bake at 350° for 45 minutes.

Hint: *I usually double this recipe and bake it in a 9"x13" pan. It always receives raves at the Seder table and throughout Passover!*

Carrot Apple Kugel

3 eggs
½ C margarine or butter
¾ C slivered almonds, divided
I apple, pared and grated
I C carrot, grated

½ C raisins
½ C matzoh meal
½ C sugar
3 T lemon juice
I tsp cinnamon

Separate eggs. Place whites in a large bowl and beat until stiff. Melt margarine or butter in a large saucepan. Remove from heat and add ½ cup of the almonds, egg yolks, apple, carrot, raisins, matzoh meal, sugar, lemon juice and cinnamon. Fold egg whites into this mixture. Pour into a greased 7"x11" or 9-inch square pan. Top with remaining ¼ cup almonds. Bake at 375° for 40 to 45 minutes, or until golden.

Passover Meringue Cookies With Mix-ins

4 egg whites
½ tsp salt
I tsp lemon juice
I tsp vanilla extract
I tsp almond extract
2 tsp lemon rind, grated

1½ C sugar
6 T cake meal
2 C walnuts, coarsely chopped
½ C coconut
I C dried fruit, chopped (dates, prunes,
   apricots, cherries, cranberries)

Beat egg whites with salt and lemon juice until soft peaks form. Add extracts and lemon rind. Gradually add sugar, beating until stiff peaks form. Combine cake meal, nuts, coconut and fruit and fold into meringue. Drop by teaspoonfuls onto parchment paper-lined cookie sheets. Bake at 350° for 12 minutes. Cool before removing from pan.

Yield: 5 dozen cookies

Hint: If you don't have parchment paper, grease the cookie sheets and dust with cake meal. These cookies are very versatile because you can vary the fruits or use any combination of fruits that you like. Chop the fruit in a food processor or cut it up with a scissors.

Passover Mandelbrot

3 eggs
1 C sugar
1 C oil
2 C cake meal
1 tsp lemon juice

Rind of 1 lemon
Chopped nuts, chocolate chips,
   raisins or combination
   of these totaling 1 C

Beat eggs and sugar. Add remaining ingredients. Allow mixture to stand at room temperature or in refrigerator for at least 40 minutes. Shape into 4 long logs, placing 2 logs on each of 2 greased cookie sheets. Bake at 350° for 25 to 30 minutes, or until golden. Remove from oven and slice. Turn slices on end and put back in oven and bake until golden, about 5 minutes.

Yield: approx. 60 pieces

Passover Kichel

$\frac{1}{4}$ C sugar
1 tsp lemon or orange rind, grated
3 eggs
$\frac{1}{2}$ C oil

1 tsp sugar
$\frac{1}{4}$ tsp salt
$\frac{1}{4}$ C potato flour
$\frac{1}{2}$ C cake meal

Combine the $\frac{1}{4}$ cup sugar and rind in a small dish and set aside. Beat eggs in an electric mixer for 5 to 10 minutes. Add oil, the 1 teaspoon sugar, and salt. Beat for an additional 10 minutes. Add potato flour and cake meal at the lowest speed of the mixer, increasing speed and beating for 5 minutes more. Drop by teaspoonfuls onto the dish of sugar and rind. Then place on foil-lined cookie sheets. Bake at 400° for 10 minutes. Reduce oven temperature to 350° and bake for 10 minutes more. Turn oven off and leave in the oven for 30 to 45 minutes.

Hint: *Do not double, because the recipe will not work properly. This is the best kichel recipe I have ever found! I make them throughout the year with leftover potato flour and cake meal (which I always have) or I substitute regular flour for the potato flour and they come out great!*

Macaroon Bars

$1\frac{1}{2}$ C walnuts or almonds
$\frac{1}{3}$ C sugar

1 to 2 egg whites, unbeaten
$\frac{3}{4}$ C jam

In a food processor, combine the nuts and sugar. Using the steel blade, process until nuts are finely ground. Through the feed tube, gradually add just enough egg white to make a firm paste. Remove the mixture from the processor and shape into 2 long rolls. Place on a greased cookie sheet. Wet your index finger and make a deep trench down the center of each roll. Bake at 350° for 15 minutes, or until light brown. While the rolls are baking, melt the jam on top of the stove or in the microwave. As soon as rolls are removed from oven, fill the trenches with melted jam. Cool. Remove rolls from cookie sheet and cut into $\frac{1}{2}$-inch diagonal slices.

Hint: By using different jams, the flavor and color of these bars may be varied. These are a tasty and unusually shaped addition to a platter of assorted pastries.

Chocolate Covered Matzoh

4 matzoh
1 C butter or margarine
1 C sugar

12 oz semi-sweet chocolate chips
Almonds, pecans or walnuts,
   chopped (optional)

Place matzoh on a greased $10\frac{1}{2}"$x$15\frac{1}{2}"$ cookie sheet. Combine butter or margarine and sugar in a saucepan and bring to a boil. Boil for 3 minutes, stirring occasionally. Pour mixture over matzoh and bake at 350° for 5 minutes. Remove from oven and immediately sprinkle chocolate chips over matzoh. Allow chocolate to melt for a few seconds. Using a spatula or knife, spread it evenly over matzoh. Sprinkle with nuts, if desired. Freeze for at least 45 minutes or refrigerate for 2 hours. Cut with serrated knife or break into pieces.

Hint: You can use half butter and half margarine in this recipe.

Passover Toffee Squares

2 sticks butter or margarine
1 C brown sugar
1 egg
1 tsp vanilla

Dash salt
1 C cake meal
8 oz chocolate chips
$\frac{1}{2}$ C walnuts, chopped

Cream butter or margarine and brown sugar until fluffy. Add egg and vanilla and beat well. Add salt and cake meal and blend well. Spread batter evenly in a greased $10\frac{1}{2}"$x$15\frac{1}{2}"$ jellyroll pan. Bake at 350° for 18 to 19 minutes, or until almost golden. Remove from oven and sprinkle with chocolate chips. Put pan back in the oven for 1 to 2 minutes, or until chocolate begins to melt. Remove from oven, and using a spatula, spread chocolate over dough until it is completely covered. Sprinkle with nuts. Cool on a wire rack and cut into squares.

Hint: To cut the recipe in half, bake in a 7"x11" pan for about 15 minutes and continue as above.

Passover Crustless Ice Cream Pie

1 qt vanilla ice cream or
   frozen yogurt
$\frac{1}{4}$ C orange juice
$\frac{3}{4}$ C medium or heavy cream, whipped

11 almond macaroons ($\frac{1}{2}$ of
   10 oz can), crumbled
$\frac{1}{2}$ C slivered almonds
10 oz pkg frozen strawberries

Let ice cream or frozen yogurt sit at room temperature until quite soft. Whisk in orange juice and cream that has been stiffly beaten. Fold in crumbled macaroons. Pour into a greased 9-inch pie plate. Sprinkle with almonds. Freeze for several hours or up to several days. Remove from freezer about 10 minutes before serving. Serve with defrosted strawberries.

Hint: You can double this recipe and pour it into a 10-inch springform pan or into a $1\frac{1}{2}$-quart bowl, in which case you would scoop it out to serve rather than slice it.

■ ■

Coconut Macaroon Pie Crust

Coconut macaroon cookies to   3 T margarine or butter
  equal 1⅓ C crumbs

Place cookies in a food processor and process finely with the steel blade until finely chopped. Cut the butter or margarine into chunks and process until the mixture is blended into a workable paste, about 5 seconds. Press into a 9-inch pie plate. Bake at 300° for 20 to 25 minutes, or until golden brown, or microwave on high for 2 minutes, or until set.

Nutty Pie Crust

2 C ground nuts (walnuts preferred)   ¼ C sugar

Place nuts in a food processor. Using the steel blade and with motor running, gradually add sugar through the feed tube. As processing continues, oil will be released from the nuts and combined with the sugar into a workable paste. Press this mixture into a 9-inch glass pie plate. Bake at 375° for 10 minutes or microwave on high for 2 minutes.

Lemon Meringue Pie Filling

Filling:

6 egg yolks   2 lemons, juice and grated rind
1 C sugar   2 egg whites, stiffly beaten

Meringue:

4 egg whites   8 T sugar

For the filling, beat yolks until light. Add sugar, lemon juice and rind. Place in a double boiler and cook until thick, stirring constantly to avoid lumps. Cool and fold in 2 of the egg whites. Pour the mixture into a crust (see above recipes). For the meringue, beat the remaining 4 egg whites until foamy. Gradually add the 8 tablespoons of sugar, 2 at a time. Continue beating until whites are stiff. Spread over pie filling and bake in 400° oven for 5 to 10 minutes.

Passover Lemon Roll

Cake:

4 eggs, separated
$\frac{2}{3}$ C granulated sugar, divided
4 tsp lemon juice
$\frac{1}{2}$ tsp lemon rind, chopped

$\frac{1}{3}$ C potato starch
$\frac{1}{3}$ C cake meal
Dash salt
$\frac{1}{3}$ C confectioners' sugar

Grease a $10\frac{1}{2}$"x$15\frac{1}{2}$" jellyroll pan. Cover with wax paper and grease the paper well. In the large bowl of an electric mixer, beat egg whites until soft peaks form when beater is slowly raised. Continue to beat, gradually adding $\frac{1}{3}$ cup of the granulated sugar, until stiff peaks form. Set aside. In the small bowl of the mixer, beat the egg yolks at high speed until they are thick and lemon-colored. Add remaining $\frac{1}{3}$ cup granulated sugar, beating constantly. Stir in lemon juice and rind. Fold this mixture into the beaten whites. Combine potato starch, cake meal and salt and fold into egg mixture, half at a time, until just blended. Do not overmix. Spread batter into prepared jellyroll pan. Bake at 350° for 12 to 13 minutes, or until a toothpick, inserted in the center, comes out clean. Remove from oven and cool for 5 minutes in the pan. Sprinkle confectioners' sugar onto a towel and turn cake out onto it. Roll up the cake and towel together from the long end. Let cool completely on a wire rack. Refrigerate (rolled up) while you make the filling.

Lemon Filling:

1 C sugar
3 T potato starch
Pinch salt
1 C water

3 egg yolks
Rind of 1 lemon, finely chopped
$\frac{1}{4}$ C lemon juice (juice of 1 lemon)
1 T margarine

In a saucepan or double boiler, combine sugar, potato starch and salt and water. Stir in egg yolks, lemon rind and juice. Cool and stir over medium heat until bubbly. Boil for only 1 minute. Remove from heat, and add the margarine. Cool before spreading onto cake roll. To fill the cake, remove it from refrigerator, unroll it and remove the towel. Spread filling evenly over the entire surface of the cake. Roll up and place on a serving platter.

Yield: $1\frac{1}{3}$ cups lemon filling

continued on next page

Passover Lemon Roll (continued)

Frosting:

1 C medium or heavy cream
2 to 3 T vanilla sugar (granulated sugar that has
  a piece of vanilla bean added to flavor it)

To make frosting, whip cream with sugar until stiff. Using a spatula, frost cake roll. If you desire, put some of the cream in a pastry bag and decorate the cake roll. Chill until serving time.

Hint: To make **Vanilla Sugar**, *fill a clean, empty jar with granulated sugar. Break a vanilla bean in half and place it in the sugar. Cover the jar tightly and within a day or two the vanilla flavor will have permeated the sugar. Vanilla sugar can be used in any recipe that contains both vanilla and sugar. It is especially nice when used in whipped cream because the cream remains white, whereas adding brown vanilla extract might make the whipped cream beige. Vanilla sugar will keep very well in a jar for many months.*

Passover Apple Cake

5 tart apples, peeled, cored and sliced
$\frac{1}{2}$ to $\frac{3}{4}$ C sugar
1 T cinnamon
Juice of 1 lemon
6 eggs

2 C sugar
1 C oil
2 C cake meal
2 T potato starch
Dash salt

Topping:

$\frac{1}{2}$ C sugar
2 tsp cinnamon

$\frac{1}{4}$ C walnuts, chopped (optional)

Grease a 9"x13" pan. Combine apples, sugar, cinnamon and lemon juice. Set aside. Beat eggs, sugar and oil together. Combine cake meal, potato starch and salt. Add to egg mixture and mix well. Pour half the batter in the pan. With a slotted spoon, remove the apples from their bowl, reserving the juices. Spread apples over batter. Pour remaining batter over apples. Combine topping ingredients and sprinkle over batter. Bake at 350° for 30 minutes. Sprinkle reserved juices from apple mixture over cake to make cake moist. Bake for an additional 10 to 15 minutes, or until a toothpick, inserted in the center, comes out clean.

■ ■

Passover Chocolate Torte

Cake:

$\frac{1}{3}$ C plus 1 T cocoa, divided
$\frac{1}{4}$ C boiling water
2 T butter or margarine, softened
1 tsp vanilla
6 eggs, separated

$\frac{2}{3}$ C sugar, divided
$\frac{1}{3}$ C blanched almonds, toasted
  and finely ground
Fresh berries, for garnish
Fresh berries, for garnish

In a small bowl, whisk together $\frac{1}{3}$ cup of the cocoa and water until smooth. Add butter or margarine and vanilla and mix until well blended. In a large bowl, combine egg yolks and $\frac{1}{2}$ cup of the sugar. Beat on medium speed until thick and light colored, about 5 minutes. Fold in cocoa mixture and almonds. In another large bowl, beat egg whites until foamy. Gradually add remaining sugar, beating until stiff peaks form. Fold one-quarter of the white mixture into the chocolate mixture. Gently fold in remaining white mixture. Pour into a $10\frac{1}{2}$"x$15\frac{1}{2}$" jellyroll pan that has been well- greased and lined with parchment paper, foil or wax paper that has also been well- greased. Bake at 350° for 18 to 20 minutes, or until cake springs back when lightly touched. Place on a wire rack to cool. Sprinkle remaining tablespoon of cocoa over cake. Cover with a clean towel and cool in pan. When cool, turn pan over and peel off parchment, foil or wax paper. With a serrated knife, cut cake into 4 equal pieces. Prepare filling, reserving $1\frac{1}{2}$ cups to frost the top and sides of torte. Place 1 layer on serving dish and spread with $\frac{1}{2}$ cup of the remaining filling. Repeat layering cake and $\frac{1}{2}$ cup cream filling. Frost top layer and sides with reserved filling. Garnish with fresh berries on top and/or extra slivered almonds.

Cocoa Whipped Cream Filling:

$1\frac{1}{2}$ C whipping cream
$\frac{1}{3}$ C sugar

3 T cocoa
$\frac{3}{4}$ tsp vanilla

In a large cold bowl, combine cream, sugar, cocoa and vanilla. Beat until stiff.

Hint: *To toast almonds, bake at 350° for 6 to 7 minutes, or until golden. Cool and grind in a food processor or blender.*

■ ■

DESSERTS

Kugelhopf
(German Coffee Cake)

5 eggs
$\frac{1}{2}$ lb butter or margarine
2 C sugar
1 tsp vanilla
$\frac{1}{4}$ C orange juice
Juice of half a lemon (2 T)
Rind of 1 lemon, grated

2 C flour
2 tsp baking powder
1 to 2 T flour
$\frac{1}{2}$ C raisins
$\frac{1}{2}$ C chocolate chips
Confectioners' sugar, for sprinkling on top

Separate eggs. Place yolks in a small bowl. Set aside. In a large mixing bowl, beat whites until stiff and set aside. In another mixing bowl, cream butter or margarine and sugar until fluffy. Add egg yolks, vanilla, juices and lemon rind. Mix 2 cups flour and baking powder together and add to yolk mixture alternately with beaten egg whites. Roll the raisins and chocolate chips in the extra 1 to 2 tablespoons flour just until they are coated. Gently fold them into the batter. Pour into a greased and floured bundt or 10-inch tube pan and bake at 350° for 45 minutes, or until a toothpick, inserted in the center, comes out clean. If you prefer, use a 6-cup kugelhopf (fluted) pan. However, it will only hold about two-thirds of the batter, so bake the remaining batter in a 9"x5" loaf pan. If using smaller pans reduce the baking time. Cool before removing from pan. Sprinkle with confectioners' sugar before serving.

Hint: *Here is a wonderful hint from my father who was a professional baker. Dad said, "If you have difficulty getting a cake out of a pan because it is sticking, just place the pan on top of your stove burner (gas or electric) for about 1 to 2 minutes. Take it off the heat and then invert the cake onto a platter. You may have to shake it a little, but the cake always comes out!!" Thanks Dad!*

Simple Versatile Cake

$\frac{1}{2}$ C butter or margarine   1 C flour
$\frac{7}{8}$ C sugar   1 tsp baking powder
2 eggs

Cream butter or margarine and sugar until fluffy. Add eggs and beat well. Fold in flour and baking powder just until blended. Spread batter in a greased 9-inch springform pan and add topping of your choice. Bake at 350° for 50 to 55 minutes, or until a toothpick, inserted in the center, comes out clean.

Toppings:

Cherry Chocolate Chip Cake

$\frac{1}{3}$ C mini-chocolate chips   Confectioners' sugar, for
$\frac{3}{4}$ to 1 C pitted canned cherries, drained   sprinkling on top
  well and wiped with a paper towel

Fold mini-chocolate chips into batter. Place cherries on top of batter in concentric circles, about $\frac{1}{2}$ inch apart. Bake as directed. When baked, cherries will sink into batter. When cool, sprinkle with confectioners' sugar.

Apple Cake

2 to $2\frac{1}{2}$ large apples, peeled and cored, $\frac{1}{2}$ tsp cinnamon
  cut into 20 slices   2 T apricot jam

Place apples in concentric circles on top of batter. Sprinkle with cinnamon. Bake as directed. Melt apricot jam in microwave for about 40 seconds on high or in a saucepan on the stove. Using a pastry brush, brush jam over apples as a glaze.

Plum Cake

14 Italian prune plums, $\frac{1}{4}$ C sugar
  halved and pitted   1 T lemon juice
$\frac{1}{2}$ tsp cinnamon

Place plums, skin-side up, over batter. Combine sugar and cinnamon and sprinkle over the plums. Drizzle lemon juice on top. Bake as directed.

■ ■

Peach Upside-Down Cake

Topping:

$\frac{1}{2}$ C brown sugar

1 T butter or margarine, softened

2 C peach slices, fresh or
canned, well drained

Grease or spray an 8-inch pan with nonstick cooking spray. Combine brown sugar and butter or margarine and pat into bottom of the cake pan. Arrange peaches on top.

Cake:

$1\frac{1}{4}$ C flour

$1\frac{1}{4}$ tsp baking powder

Dash salt

$\frac{3}{4}$ C sugar

2 eggs

$\frac{1}{4}$ C butter or margarine, softened

$\frac{2}{3}$ C milk

1 tsp vanilla

Combine all ingredients in a large mixing bowl and blend on low speed until well mixed. Turn mixer onto high speed and continue mixing for 3 to 4 minutes, or until everything is well blended. Pour batter over peaches. Bake at 350° for 35 to 40 minutes, or until a toothpick, inserted in the center, comes out clean. Cool cake in pan for about 10 minutes. Invert onto a serving plate. Serve warm, garnished with ice cream, frozen yogurt or whipped cream, if desired.

Hint: *Although this is best when served warm, it is still tasty at room temperature.*

Cheese Cake Cookie Squares

$\frac{1}{3}$ C brown sugar, packed

$\frac{1}{2}$ C walnuts, chopped

1 C flour

$\frac{1}{2}$ C butter or margarine, softened

8 oz pkg cream cheese

$\frac{1}{4}$ C sugar

1 egg

1 T lemon juice

2 T cream or milk

Combine brown sugar, nuts and flour in a large bowl. Stir in butter or margarine and mix with your hands until crumbly. Remove 1 cup of mixture and reserve. Place remainder in an 8-inch square pan and press firmly. Bake at 350° for 12 to 15 minutes. Beat cream cheese and sugar until smooth. Add egg, lemon juice, cream or milk and vanilla and mix well. Pour this onto baked crust. Top with reserved crumbs. Return to oven and bake for an additional 25 minutes. Cool and cut into squares. Cover with plastic wrap and refrigerate.

■ ■

Orange Sponge Cake

6 eggs, separated
1½ C sugar, divided
1¾ C flour, sifted
Dash salt

6 T fresh orange juice
Rind of 1 orange, grated
Confectioners' sugar, for
   sprinkling on top

In a large bowl of an electric mixer, beat the egg whites at medium speed until they are foamy. Gradually beat in ½ cup of the sugar, beating after each addition. Continue beating until stiff peaks form. Set aside. In a small bowl of an electric mixer, beat the yolks, at high speed, until they are very thick and lemon-colored. Do not underbeat. Gradually add the remaining sugar until the mixture is smooth. At low speed, beat in the flour and salt alternately with the orange juice, beginning and ending with flour. Add orange rind. With a rubber scraper, gently fold the yolk mixture into the whites. Pour the batter into an <u>ungreased</u> 10"x4½" tube pan <u>without</u> a removable bottom. Bake at 350° for 35 to 40 minutes, or until the cake springs back when pressed with a finger. Invert cake over a narrow-neck bottle so that the top of the bottle sticks through the opening in the pan and holds the cake up to cool. Cool completely before removing from the pan. Sprinkle with confectioners' sugar.

Hint: *If you don't want such a large cake, you can cut this recipe in half and bake it in an ungreased kugelhopf (4-cup) or small bundt pan.*

Triple Berry Cake

¼ C butter or margarine
¾ C sugar
1 egg
¾ C milk
1 tsp vanilla
2 C flour

2 tsp baking powder
½ tsp salt
¾ C blueberries
¾ C raspberries
¾ C strawberries, hulled and sliced

Topping:

⅓ C sugar

1 tsp butter or margarine, melted

Cream butter or margarine with sugar and egg until fluffy. Add milk and vanilla. Blend in flour, baking powder and salt. Gently fold in berries by hand. Pour into a greased 9-inch square or round pan. Combine the ingredients for topping and drizzle over cake. Bake at 375° for 35 to 40 minutes, or until a toothpick, inserted in the center, comes out clean. Cool on a wire rack.

Hint: *You can use frozen berries, but do not thaw before adding to the batter.*

■ ■

Cream Puffs

1 C water	1 C flour
$\frac{1}{2}$ C butter or margarine	4 eggs

In a medium saucepan, heat water and butter or margarine until boiling. Remove from heat. With a wooden spoon, beat in the flour all at once. Return to low heat, and continue beating until mixture forms a ball and leaves the sides of the pan. Remove from heat. Cool slightly and add eggs, one at a time, beating after each addition, until mixture is smooth. For large cream puffs, drop heaping tablespoonfuls (about $\frac{1}{3}$ cup) of dough onto greased cookie sheets. For tiny cream puffs, drop by teaspoonfuls or through a pastry tube in 1- to 1$\frac{1}{2}$-inch mounds onto greased sheets. Flatten pointed tops with the back of a wet spoon or your moistened finger tip. Bake at 425° for 15 minutes. Reduce heat to 350° and bake an additional 15 to 20 minutes, or until puffs are golden. Cool on a wire rack. To serve, cut in half and fill with ice cream, frozen yogurt, custard or whipped cream. If filling with ice cream or frozen yogurt, serve with **Ice Cream Parlor Hot Fudge Sauce** (see pg. 191). If filling with custard or whipped cream, frost with chocolate or colored icing.

Yield: 8 or 9 large or 48 to 54 small cream puffs

Hint: *These puffs can be made far in advance and frozen. To recrisp them, bake at 250° for 7 to 10 minutes. Cream puffs can also be filled with tuna, egg, or seafood salad.*

Finnish Spice Cake

$\frac{1}{2}$ C butter, melted, divided	1 tsp baking soda
2 T bread crumbs	2 tsp cinnamon
2 eggs	$\frac{1}{2}$ tsp cloves
1 C sour cream	$\frac{1}{2}$ tsp cardamom
2 C flour	Rind of 1 orange, grated
2 C sugar	

Melt butter. Dip a pastry brush into butter and brush all over the inside of a bundt pan. Sprinkle pan with bread crumbs. Beat eggs and add sour cream. Sift all the dry ingredients and add to egg mixture. Fold in orange rind and remaining melted butter, just until blended. Pour into prepared pan and bake at 350° for 45 minutes, or until a toothpick, inserted in the center, comes out clean.

Hint: *This can also be baked in (3) 3"x6" mini-loaf pans for 30 to 35 minutes, or until a toothpick, inserted in the center, comes out clean.*

Sour Cream Coffee Cake

Featured in Cover Photo

$2\frac{1}{2}$ C flour
$\frac{1}{2}$ tsp baking powder
1 tsp baking soda
Pinch salt
3 eggs, separated

$1\frac{1}{2}$ C sugar, divided
1 C butter or margarine
1 C sour cream
2 tsp vanilla

Topping:

$\frac{1}{2}$ C walnuts
$\frac{1}{4}$ C brown sugar

3 T cinnamon
4 oz bar German's sweet chocolate

Sift together flour, baking powder, baking soda and salt. Separate eggs, putting yolks into a small bowl and whites into a medium bowl. Add $\frac{1}{2}$ cup of the sugar to the whites and beat until fairly thick. Set aside. In a large bowl, cream together butter or margarine and remaining 1 cup sugar until smooth. Add egg yolks, one at a time, beating well after each addition. Add dry ingredients alternately with sour cream, beating well after each addition. Add vanilla and mix. Slowly fold in reserved egg whites, just until blended. Pour half of batter into a greased and floured 10-inch bundt or tube pan. Combine topping ingredients in a food processor until chocolate is grated and nuts are finely chopped. Sprinkle over batter in pan. Spread remaining batter on top. Bake at 350° for 50 to 55 minutes, or until a toothpick, inserted in the center, comes out clean.

Hint: *This is a rich traditional cake that is wonderful any time of the day. It freezes well.*

Chocolate Cheese Cake

Crust:

$1\frac{3}{4}$ C chocolate cookie crumbs

$\frac{1}{2}$ tsp cinnamon

2 T brown sugar

$\frac{1}{2}$ C butter or margarine, melted

Combine all ingredients, reserving $\frac{1}{3}$ cup of the mixture to sprinkle over the filling before it is baked. Press crumb mixture over the bottom of a greased 9-inch springform pan.

Filling:

12 oz chocolate chips

1 lb cream cheese

$\frac{3}{4}$ C sugar

4 eggs

$\frac{1}{2}$ C sour cream

Melt chocolate chips in a double boiler or microwave. Cool. In a large bowl, combine cream cheese and sugar and beat until fluffy. Add eggs, one at a time, beating after each addition. Add sour cream and mix until well blended. Pour over crust and sprinkle with reserved crumb mixture. Bake at 350° for 50 to 55 minutes. The edges of the cake will be set, but the center will be somewhat runny. Turn the oven off and let the cake cool for 30 minutes with the oven door partly open. The surface of the cake may crack slightly. When the cake is completely cool, remove the sides of the pan and transfer to a serving plate.

Topping:

$\frac{1}{2}$ C whipping cream

1 T confectioners' sugar

Whip cream until fairly stiff. Add confectioners' sugar and beat until stiff. Transfer to a pastry bag fitted with a star tube. Garnish cake with rosettes of whipped cream. Garnish each rosette with a chocolate chip or fresh raspberry.

Hint: *To reduce fat, use light cream cheese and reduced fat sour cream. With or without the cream, this is especially tasty served with* **Three Berry Medley** *(pg. 184) poured over each piece of cake.*

Italian Ricotta Cheese Cake

Filling:

2 lbs ricotta cheese
$\frac{2}{3}$ C sugar
6 eggs

2 tsp vanilla
Rind of 1 orange, grated

Beat cheese and sugar at medium speed for 3 to 4 minutes, or until well blended. Add eggs one at a time, beating after each addition. Fold in vanilla and orange rind. Do not preheat oven before baking.

Crust:

2 C flour
$\frac{2}{3}$ C sugar
Pinch salt

$\frac{3}{4}$ C butter, at room temperature
1 egg

Combine flour, sugar and salt in a large bowl. Make a well in the center and place butter in it. With floured hands, work butter into flour mixture until pebbly. Add egg and mix in with a fork. Using your hands, shape the dough into a smooth ball. Cut off a quarter of the dough and set it aside. On a floured surface, using a rolling pin, roll out the remaining dough into small sections. Press these into the bottom and all the way up the sides of a 9-inch springform pan. Pour filling into pan. Roll out remaining dough into long strips, cutting dough with a pastry wheel. Weave strips in and out, as well as possible, on top of the filling. The overlapping of dough strips is important; otherwise the dough strips will become submerged as the cake bakes. Place cake in an unheated oven and turn oven to 350°. Bake for 70 minutes, or until top begins to get a little golden. Cool on a wire rack completely before removing from the pan. Serve at room temperature. Refrigerate, if not serving immediately.

Hint: *This cake tastes best when made 1 to 2 days before serving. The cake traditionally is made with whole milk or full cream ricotta; however, it is still delicious if part skim ricotta is used.*

Walnut Roll With Cappuccino Cream

Roll:

6 eggs
1 C sugar, divided
2 tsp baking powder
1 tsp vanilla

1 C walnuts, finely ground
1 to 2 T confectioners' sugar, for
   sprinkling on cooled cake

Separate eggs and place yolks in the small bowl and whites in the large bowl of an electric mixer. Grease bottom and sides of a $10\frac{1}{2}"$x$15\frac{1}{2}"$ jellyroll pan. Line with wax paper and grease paper. Set aside. Beat whites until foamy. Gradually add $\frac{1}{2}$ cup of the sugar and continue beating until whites are stiff and glossy. Set aside. In a small bowl, beat egg yolks with the remaining sugar for 5 minutes, or until mixture becomes thick and lemon-colored. Beat in baking powder, vanilla and ground nuts just until blended. Gently fold in egg whites just until blended. Do not overmix. Pour batter into prepared pan. Bake at 350° for 20 minutes, or until top seems dry. Remove from oven and immediately cover with a dish towel. When cool, refrigerate until ready to fill and frost. When ready to fill and frost, sprinkle confectioners' sugar over the cake and invert it onto a large sheet of wax paper.

Cappuccino Cream Filling and Frosting

$1\frac{1}{2}$ C whipping cream
1 T instant espresso or coffee granules
$2\frac{1}{2}$ T sugar

1 T cocoa
1 T Kahlua or other coffee liqueur

Combine cream, espresso or coffee, sugar, cocoa and Kahlua and beat until stiff. Peel wax paper off the cake. Spread about two-thirds of the filling over the cake. Using a new piece of wax paper to help you, roll the cake lengthwise, ending with the seam-side down. Place on a serving plate. Frost with remaining cream. Decorate with chocolate chips or chocolate-covered coffee beans. Refrigerate for at least 1 hour before serving. To serve, slice with a serrated knife.

Hint: *You can bake the cake up to 2 days in advance of frosting it. You can completely finish it one day ahead by keeping it refrigerated.*

■ ■

Blueberry Buckle

$\frac{1}{2}$ C butter or margarine	2 C flour
$\frac{3}{4}$ C sugar	$\frac{1}{2}$ tsp salt
1 egg	1 T baking powder
$\frac{1}{2}$ C milk	2 C blueberries

Crumb Topping:

$\frac{1}{2}$ C sugar	$\frac{1}{4}$ C butter or margarine, softened
$\frac{1}{3}$ C flour	$\frac{1}{2}$ tsp cinnamon

Cream butter or margarine and sugar until fluffy. Add egg and blend well. Stir in milk, flour, salt and baking powder. Fold in blueberries and mix until blended. Pour into a greased and floured 9-inch square pan. In a small bowl, combine topping ingredients and blend with a fork. Sprinkle topping over cake. Bake at 350° for 45 minutes, or until a toothpick, inserted in the center, comes out clean.

Almond Poppy Seed Cake

1 C butter or margarine	$\frac{1}{2}$ tsp salt
$1\frac{1}{2}$ C sugar	1 C buttermilk or yogurt
4 eggs, separated	1 tsp almond extract
$2\frac{1}{2}$ C flour	3 T poppy seeds
1 tsp baking soda	$\frac{1}{2}$ C sliced almonds
2 tsp baking powder	

In a large bowl, cream butter or margarine and sugar until light and fluffy. Add egg yolks and mix well. Sift together the flour, baking soda, baking powder and salt. Add this to the creamed mixture, alternately with the buttermilk or yogurt. Add the almond extract and poppy seeds and mix just until blended. In a small bowl, beat the egg whites until stiff. Fold into the batter. Grease and flour a bundt pan and sprinkle the almonds over the bottom of the pan. Pour the batter over the almonds and bake at 350° for 45 to 50 minutes, or until a toothpick, inserted in the center, comes out clean. Cool in the pan for 15 minutes and turn out onto a wire rack to finish cooling.

Hint: *This is a delicious moist cake which, if tightly wrapped, will keep well at room temperature for a couple of days. It also freezes well.*

Poppy Seed Cake

$\frac{1}{2}$ C poppy seeds
$\frac{3}{4}$ C warm water
2 eggs plus 1 additional egg white
$\frac{3}{4}$ C butter or margarine
$1\frac{1}{2}$ C sugar

1 tsp vanilla or almond extract
2 C flour
2 tsp baking powder
Dash salt

Soak poppy seeds in water and set aside. Separate eggs. Beat 3 egg whites until stiff. Cream butter or margarine with sugar until fluffy. Add egg yolks and mix. Add extract. Fold in poppy seed and water mixture. Sift flour, baking powder and salt and add to batter. Fold in beaten egg whites, a third at a time. Pour into a greased and floured bundt or tube pan and bake at 375° for 35 to 40 minutes, or until a toothpick, inserted in the center, comes out clean.

Hint: *You can make a* **Lemon Poppy Seed Cake** *by substituting 1 teaspoon lemon extract for the vanilla or almond and adding the finely chopped rind of 1 lemon. Use the same procedure to make* **Orange Poppy Seed Cake**, *substituting orange extract and orange rind. You can also bake this cake in a 9"x5" loaf pan or (2) 3"x6" mini-pans. However, reduce baking time if using mini-pans.*

Cranapple Coffee Cake

$1\frac{1}{2}$ C sugar, divided
2 tsp cinnamon
$1\frac{1}{2}$ C (6 oz) cranberries,
  coarsely chopped
3 apples, thinly sliced
$\frac{1}{2}$ C butter or margarine
2 eggs

1 tsp vanilla
2 C flour
1 tsp baking powder
1 tsp baking soda
1 C sour cream
$\frac{1}{2}$ C walnuts, chopped (optional)

Mix $\frac{1}{2}$ cup of the sugar with cinnamon and sprinkle over cranberries and apples. Set aside. Cream butter or margarine with remaining sugar. Add eggs and vanilla. Combine flour, baking powder and baking soda and add alternately with sour cream. Fold in walnuts, if desired. Spread half the batter in a greased tube or Bundt pan. Spread fruit mixture on top. Spread with remaining batter. Bake at 375° for 55 to 60 minutes, or until a toothpick, inserted in the center, comes out clean.

Hint: *To reduce fat, substitute low fat sour cream or yogurt for the sour cream.*

Sesame Cookies

$\frac{2}{3}$ C butter

$\frac{3}{4}$ C sugar

2 egg yolks

1 T anise or almond extract

$\frac{1}{4}$ C milk

2 C flour

$1\frac{1}{2}$ tsp baking powder

$\frac{1}{4}$ tsp salt

$\frac{1}{2}$ tsp sesame seeds

1 C sesame seeds, for rolling out dough

Cream butter and sugar until fluffy. Add egg yolks and extract and blend well. Add milk, flour, baking powder, salt and $\frac{1}{2}$ teaspoon sesame seeds. Knead or mix until smooth. Refrigerate dough for about 1 hour, or until firm enough to shape into logs. Remove from refrigerator and shape dough into 1- to $1\frac{1}{2}$-inch logs. Sprinkle sesame seeds on a bread board or kitchen counter and roll dough logs in sesame seeds. Using a knife, diagonally slice dough into 1-inch pieces. Turn pieces on their sides and roll in seeds so that seeds will cover all surfaces of dough. Place pieces of dough on greased cookie sheets and bake at 350° for 17 to 20 minutes, or until edges are golden. Cool on wire racks.

Yield: 60 cookies

Hint: *This is a traditional Italian cookie which my neighbor's mother always makes during the holiday season. My family loves these cookies so much that I said, "I must have this recipe!"*

Spiced Nuts

$\frac{1}{2}$ C sugar

$\frac{1}{2}$ tsp cinnamon

$\frac{1}{4}$ tsp nutmeg

$\frac{1}{8}$ tsp allspice

3 C (12 oz) hazelnuts, almonds

   or pecans

1 egg white, lightly beaten

Combine sugar and spices. Toss nuts around in egg white until well coated. Then roll in sugar and spice mixture. Spread on a cookie sheet. Bake at 350° for 15 minutes, shaking pan a few times. When nuts are removed from oven, use a fork to separate them. Cool on a wire rack.

Yield: spiced nuts to fill (4) 8-ounce jars

Hint: *You can use a combination of nuts if you like. These are delicious to serve along with hors d'oeuvres or they can be served with dessert. If placed in decorative jars or tins, they make wonderful gifts.*

Chocolate Mint Candy Cookies

$\frac{3}{4}$ C butter or margarine

$1\frac{1}{2}$ C dark brown sugar, packed

2 T water

12 oz semi-sweet chocolate chips

2 eggs

$2\frac{1}{2}$ C flour

$1\frac{1}{4}$ tsp baking soda

$\frac{3}{4}$ lb green chocolate mint wafer candies

Place butter or margarine, brown sugar and water in a large bowl. Microwave for 2 to 3 minutes on medium-high, or until melted. Add chocolate chips and microwave for 1 to 2 minutes more, or until melted. If not completely melted, stir until it is. Transfer mixture to a mixing bowl and cool for 10 minutes. Beat in eggs, 1 at a time. Add dry ingredients and mix until well blended. Chill dough for at least one hour. When ready to bake, cover 2 cookie sheets with foil. Roll teaspoonfuls of dough into 1-inch balls and place 2 inches apart on cookie sheets. Bake at 350° for 13 to 14 minutes. Remove from oven and immediately place a mint wafer on each cookie. Transfer to wire racks. Cookies will crisp as they cool. Allow candy to soften and begin melting. Using your finger, move mint around to swirl over cookie. Transfer to a wire rack and cool completely. It may take about 35 to 45 minutes for the swirled chocolate to harden. These freeze well.

Yield: 6 dozen cookies

Hermits

$\frac{1}{2}$ C butter or margarine

$1\frac{1}{4}$ C sugar

1 egg

$\frac{1}{4}$ C molasses

$\frac{1}{3}$ C water

3 C flour

Dash salt

$1\frac{1}{2}$ tsp baking soda

$\frac{1}{2}$ tsp cloves

$\frac{1}{2}$ tsp ginger

$\frac{1}{2}$ tsp cinnamon

$\frac{1}{2}$ C raisins

$\frac{1}{2}$ C walnuts, chopped (optional)

Cream butter or margarine with sugar until fluffy. Add egg, molasses and water. Beat well. Add all dry ingredients and mix. Add raisins and nuts. Spread (2) 1-inch strips of batter on each of 3 greased cookie sheets. Bake at 350° for 20 to 22 minutes. Remove from oven. Using a serrated knife, slice on the diagonal into $1\frac{1}{2}$- to 2-inch pieces. Using a metal spatula, move the pieces to wire racks to cool.

Yield: 60 hermits

Hint: *If you prefer larger hermits, make wider slices. If you don't want to add nuts, increase raisins to 1 cup. These keep well in a tin.*

Chocolate Slice-and-Bake Cookies

Featured in Cover Photo

$\frac{1}{2}$ C butter or margarine, softened
1 C sugar
1 egg
1 tsp vanilla

$1\frac{1}{3}$ C flour
$\frac{1}{2}$ C unsweetened cocoa
$\frac{3}{4}$ tsp baking soda
$\frac{1}{4}$ tsp salt

Cream butter or margarine, sugar, egg and vanilla until light and fluffy. Combine flour, cocoa, baking soda and salt. Blend into creamed mixture. Divide dough in half. With floured hands, shape each half into a long roll, $1\frac{1}{2}$ inches in diameter. Wrap in plastic wrap. Chill for several hours, or overnight. Cut each roll into $\frac{1}{4}$-inch slices. Place on ungreased cookie sheets. Bake at 375° for 7 to 8 minutes, or until almost set. Cool for 30 seconds and then remove from cookie sheets to a wire rack.

Yield: 8 dozen cookies

Hint: *These rolls of cookie dough may be frozen for a few months and then removed from the freezer and baked as needed. They don't even have to be defrosted before baking. To make cookies more festive looking, you can place some mini-M&Ms or colored sprinkles on top before baking.*

Pecan Squares

$\frac{1}{2}$ C butter or margarine
1 C dark brown sugar
1 egg
$\frac{1}{2}$ tsp vanilla
1 C flour

$\frac{1}{2}$ tsp baking powder
Dash salt
1 C pecans, coarsely broken
Confectioners' sugar, for sprinkling on top

Using an electric mixer, cream butter or margarine and brown sugar until fluffy. Add egg and vanilla. Beat well. Fold in flour, baking powder and salt. Remove the bowl from the mixer and stir in pecans with a spoon. Spread batter in a greased 9-inch square pan. Bake at 350° for 25 to 28 minutes, or just until the middle of the dough is set, and a toothpick, inserted in the center, comes out clean. Cool on a wire rack and cut into squares. Sprinkle with confectioners' sugar.

Hint: *These squares can be cut into large 4- or 5-inch pieces and topped with vanilla ice cream or frozen yogurt to serve as dessert or they can be cut into 2-inch squares and served like a cookie or small pastry. They freeze well.*

■ ■

Fabulous Crispy Oatmeal Cookies

1 C granulated sugar
1 C dark brown sugar
2 C oatmeal
2 C flour
$\frac{1}{2}$ tsp salt
1 tsp baking soda
1 tsp baking powder

2 eggs
1 C butter or margarine, melted
1 tsp vanilla
Optional Mix-ins:
   Add 1 C or a mixture of the following:
   nuts, raisins, coconut or chopped dates

Combine sugars and oatmeal. Sift flour with salt, baking soda and baking powder. Add to oatmeal mixture. Beat eggs and add to dry ingredients. Add melted butter or margarine and mix well. Add vanilla. Add "mix-ins," if desired. Place tablespoons of batter onto ungreased cookie sheets. These spread, so only place 9 cookies on a sheet. Bake at 350° for 12 to 15 minutes, or until crisp and golden. Immediately remove from pan and place on wire racks to cool.

Hint: *One of my sons, who claims to be an oatmeal cookie expert, rates these as "the incredibly best oatmeal cookies!"*

Mincemeat Cookies

1 C butter or margarine, softened
2 C sugar
1 egg
2 C flour

Dash salt
$\frac{1}{2}$ tsp baking soda
1 tsp vanilla
9 oz pkg concentrated mincemeat

Cream butter or margarine and sugar until fluffy. Add egg and mix well. Add flour, salt, baking soda and vanilla and mix until well blended. Fold in mincemeat. Dough may be refrigerated at this point, covered, for up to 24 hours. To bake, roll dough into 1-inch balls and place on parchment paper or foil-lined cookie sheets about 2 inches apart. Do not put more than 12 cookies on a sheet because they spread. Bake at 350° for 12 to 14 minutes, or until golden. After removing cookie sheets from the oven, allow cookies to remain on sheets for 30 to 60 seconds before transferring onto cooling racks.

Yield: 5 to $5\frac{1}{2}$ dozen cookies

Hint: *Before tasting these cookies, mincemeat never appealed to me. However, once I tasted these cookies, I quickly changed my mind!*

Rocky Road Brownies

$\frac{3}{4}$ C butter or margarine
2 squares unsweetened chocolate
1 C sugar
1 C flour

Dash salt
2 eggs
1 tsp vanilla
$\frac{3}{4}$ to 1 C walnuts, chopped (optional)

Topping:

28 marshmallows
12 oz chocolate chips

$\frac{1}{2}$ C milk

Melt butter or margarine and chocolate together and add remaining ingredients, except for topping. Bake in a greased 9"x13" pan at 350° for 12 minutes (brownies will be underbaked). Remove from oven. Place marshmallows on top in rows of 4 across and 7 down. Bake for an additional 5 minutes. While brownies are baking, melt chocolate chips over a double boiler and whisk in the milk, until smooth. Spread over the brownies. Cool for at least 30 minutes. Refrigerate until firm. Cut into squares.

Hint: *To cut the brownies, use a serrated knife. Dip knife into hot water after every few cuts or marshmallow will stick to knife. These brownies freeze well.*

Double Chocolate Chip Cookies

1 C butter or margarine
1 C granulated sugar
$\frac{1}{2}$ C brown sugar, firmly packed
1 tsp vanilla
1 egg
2 T milk

$\frac{1}{3}$ C cocoa
$1\frac{3}{4}$ C flour
$\frac{1}{4}$ tsp baking soda
1 C walnuts or pecans, coarsely chopped
6 oz semi-sweet chocolate chips or
    white chocolate chips or combination

Cream butter or margarine, both sugars and vanilla until fluffy. Add egg and milk. Add cocoa and blend well. Add flour and baking soda and mix just until blended. With a wooden spoon, fold in nuts and chocolate chips. Drop by teaspoonfuls onto greased cookie sheets. Bake at 350° for 12 to 13 minutes. Cookies will appear soft. Transfer to a wire cooling rack.

Yield: 4 dozen cookies

Pecan Snowball Cookies

$\frac{1}{2}$ lb butter or margarine
$\frac{1}{2}$ C confectioners' sugar
I tsp vanilla

2 C flour, sifted
I$\frac{1}{2}$ C pecans, finely chopped
$\frac{1}{2}$ to I C confectioners' sugar, for rolling

Beat butter or margarine with $\frac{1}{2}$ cup confectioners' sugar until fluffy. Add vanilla, flour and pecans. Shape into small balls and place on greased cookie sheets. Bake at 350° for 8 to 10 minutes, or until very light brown. Do not overbake. Roll in confectioners' sugar while hot. Cool on wire racks.

Yield: 5$\frac{1}{2}$ to 6 dozen cookies

Hint: *The easiest way to coat the cookies with the confectioners' sugar is to put the sugar on a sheet of waxed paper and roll the cookies around in it. These cookies will keep well in a tin, as long as my middle son's girlfriend isn't around to "sample" them!*

Chocolate Butterflies or Bows

Featured in Cover Photo

24 wonton wrappers
I to 2 C canola oil, for frying
6 oz semi-sweet chocolate

Confectioners' sugar, for
  sprinkling on top
I tsp canola oil

Dip your fingers in water and run them down the middle of the front and back center of each wonton wrapper. Pinch wrappers from the middle of 2 opposite edges, towards the "water stripe" to form "butterfly wings" or "bows". Heat oil in a wok or deep pot until hot, but not smoking. Fry a few "butterflies" or "bows" at a time cooking quickly until light golden in color. Turn over and fry until golden on the other side. Remove from wok or pot and drain on paper towels. Cool and sprinkle with confectioners' sugar. Melt chocolate on top of a double boiler over hot, not boiling water. Add I teaspoon oil and blend well. Dip each outer edge of "wings" or "bows" into chocolate. Drain on wire racks until chocolate is set.

Hint: *These are delicious even without the chocolate. Also you can bake the "butterflies" or "bows" rather than fry them, while still obtaining a delicious and attractive result. To bake, spray a cookie sheet with nonstick cooking spray. Shape the wontons following above directions. You can leave them plain, spray with cooking spray or brush with melted margarine or butter before baking. Bake at 400°, or until almost golden. Follow same procedures as above. Wonton wrappers are found in the produce department of the supermarket.*

Grapenut Cookies

I C butter or margarine
I C sugar
I tsp white vinegar

$1\frac{1}{2}$ C plus 2 T flour
I tsp baking soda
$\frac{1}{2}$ C grapenuts (cereal)

Cream butter or margarine with sugar until fluffy. Add remaining ingredients and mix until well blended. Drop by teaspoonfuls onto greased cookie sheets, placing a maximum of 12 cookies per sheet, because the dough spreads. Bake at 350° for 10 to 12 minutes, or until golden. Allow cookies to remain on cookie sheets for about 45 seconds before transferring to wire racks to cool.

Yield: 4 dozen cookies

Hint: *These crisp, buttery cookies keep well in a tightly sealed tin.*

Biscotti

Featured in Cover Photo

$\frac{1}{2}$ C butter or margarine
$1\frac{1}{3}$ C sugar
3 eggs
I T anise seed, toasted, or
  I tsp almond extract
Zest of I lemon, finely chopped

Zest of I orange, finely chopped
3 C flour
$2\frac{1}{2}$ tsp baking powder
$\frac{1}{2}$ tsp baking soda
2 C almonds or hazelnuts,
  coarsely chopped

Cream butter or margarine and sugar until fluffy. Add eggs, one at a time, beating after each addition. Add zests and anise seed or almond extract. Add dry ingredients. Fold in nuts. Divide dough into thirds. Roll each third into a log 12 inches long by $1\frac{1}{2}$ inches wide. Place on greased cookie sheets. With floured fingers, flatten to I inch. Bake at 325° for 25 minutes, rotating pans after 12 to 15 minutes. Cool. Using a sharp knife, slice on the diagonal. Place cut sides up on cookie sheets. Reduce oven temperature to 275° and bake for an additional 25 to 30 minutes, or until golden. Cool on wire racks.

Yield: (80) 2- to 3-inch biscotti

Hint: *If you want to make smaller biscotti, divide dough in fourths or sixths instead of thirds. Also you can coat the bottom of the baked and cooled biscotti in semi-sweet, dark or white chocolate. Melt chocolate in a double boiler, adding a few drops of canola oil or butter, just until mixture is melted and smooth. Dip bottoms of biscotti in melted chocolate. Turn upside-down on a wire rack until chocolate is set.*

■ ■

Chocolate Biscotti

$\frac{3}{4}$ C almonds or hazelnuts,
   coarsely chopped
$\frac{1}{2}$ C butter or margarine
$\frac{3}{4}$ C sugar
2 eggs
2 T Kahlua, Amaretto or strong coffee

$2\frac{1}{8}$ C flour
$\frac{1}{3}$ C cocoa
$1\frac{1}{2}$ tsp baking powder
Dash salt
$\frac{2}{3}$ C semisweet or milk chocolate, chopped

Bake nuts in a 350° oven for 9 to 10 minutes, or until golden brown. Let cool. If using hazelnuts, rub off the loose skins with your hands. Chop with a knife so that you still have fairly large pieces. Cream butter or margarine and sugar until fluffy. Beat in eggs and liqueur or coffee. Add flour, cocoa, baking powder and salt and mix until blended. Fold in nuts and chocolate. Divide dough in half and pat into 2 logs on a greased and floured cookie sheet. Bake at 325° for 25 minutes, or until lightly brown. Transfer to a wire rack and cool for 5 minutes. Using a serrated knife, slice diagonally on a 45 degree angle about $\frac{1}{2}$ inch thick. Place the slices on their sides on the cookie sheet and return to oven for 10 to 15 additional minutes to "dry" the cookies. Remove from the oven and cool on wire racks.

Yield: (4 dozen) $2\frac{1}{2}$- to 3-inch biscotti

Hint: If you want smaller biscotti, divide the dough into thirds and mound in 3 strips on the cookie sheet. Also, milk chocolate or semisweet chocolate chips may be used. Biscotti are a traditional Italian cookie that are delicious for dunking in coffee or tea. They will keep in a tin at room temperature for up to 2 weeks, or in the freezer for several months.

Italian Almond Macaroon Cookies

$1\frac{1}{2}$ C sugar
3 egg whites
$\frac{1}{2}$ lb slivered almonds

1 lb almond paste, shredded or
   broken into small pieces

Combine sugar and egg whites and mix in an electric mixer for 5 minutes. Add shredded almond paste and mix well. Roll dough into $\frac{1}{2}$-inch balls or drop by $\frac{1}{2}$ teaspoonfuls into a shallow bowl containing slivered almonds. When dough is completely covered with almonds, transfer to greased and floured cookie sheets. Bake at 350° for 15 to 20 minutes, or until cookies are slightly golden. Allow cookies to remain on cookie sheet for 1 to 2 minutes before transferring to wire cooling racks.

Yield: 5 to $5\frac{1}{2}$ dozen cookies

Date Nut Double Deckers

Crust:

$1\frac{1}{4}$ C sifted flour
$\frac{1}{3}$ C granulated sugar

$\frac{1}{2}$ C butter or margarine

Topping:

$\frac{1}{3}$ C brown sugar
$\frac{1}{3}$ C granulated sugar
2 eggs
I tsp vanilla
2 T flour
I tsp baking powder

Dash salt
$\frac{1}{4}$ tsp nutmeg
I C walnuts, chopped
8 oz dates, chopped
Confectioners' sugar, for
   sprinkling on top

Combine the ingredients for the crust and blend until it looks like fine crumbs. Press in a 9-inch square pan. Bake at 350° for 20 minutes, or until the edges are lightly browned. Combine the sugars, eggs and vanilla and beat well. Sift the flour, baking powder, salt and nutmeg and add to the egg mixture. Stir in the walnuts and dates. Pour batter over the hot crust and bake for 20 additional minutes. Cool in the pan. Dip knife in hot water to cut into squares. Sprinkle with confectioners' sugar.

Yield: 25 squares

Hint: *These are very easy to make. You can prepare the topping while the crust is baking.*

Chewy Squares

I C (6 oz) butterscotch chips
$\frac{1}{4}$ C butter or margarine
$\frac{1}{4}$ C brown sugar
I egg
$\frac{3}{4}$ C flour
I tsp baking powder

$\frac{1}{2}$ C walnuts or pecans,
   coarsely chopped
$\frac{3}{4}$ C miniature marshmallows
I tsp vanilla
$\frac{1}{2}$ C chocolate chips

In the top of a double boiler, combine butterscotch chips, butter or margarine and brown sugar and stir until melted. Remove from heat and whisk in egg. Add remaining ingredients, making sure that they are well mixed. Pour into a greased 8-inch square pan. Bake at 350° for 20 to 22 minutes, or until a toothpick, inserted in center, is dry. Cool and cut into squares.

■ ■

Apricot Squares

Crust:

$\frac{1}{2}$ C butter or margarine

$\frac{1}{4}$ C sugar

1 C flour

Combine crust ingredients in a mixer or food processor until a ball of dough forms. With floured fingertips, pat dough into a 9-inch square baking pan. Bake at 350° for 15 to 20 minutes, or until dough begins to turn golden.

Filling:

$\frac{1}{2}$ lb dried apricots, diced

$\frac{1}{2}$ C water

2 eggs

1 C sugar

$\frac{1}{2}$ tsp vanilla

$\frac{1}{2}$ C walnuts, coarsely chopped

While dough is baking, place apricots and water in a saucepan and bring to a boil. Turn heat down and simmer for 7 to 8 minutes, or until water is absorbed and apricots are tender. Cool briefly and put apricots in food processor and purée. Add eggs, sugar and vanilla and combine until mixed. Fold in nuts. Spread over partially baked crust and bake for 30 minutes. Cool on a wire rack. Cut into squares.

Hint: If you don't have a food processor or don't want to purée the cooked apricots, you can omit that step and blend apricots with remaining filling ingredients.

Dried Fruit Compote

2 C dried fruit such as apricots, peaches, prunes, cherries, mangoes or cranberries

1 cinnamon stick

3 C water

Place fruit and cinnamon stick in a pot and cover with water. Bring water to a boil and turn off heat. Cover pot and allow mixture to cool. Refrigerate for several hours or overnight.

Hint: To save time, cook this in a Corningware pan. Cool and refrigerate for up to a week. This can be served out of the same pan. For guests, you may want to serve the compote in champagne glasses or pretty dessert dishes. Dried fruit is fat free and high in fiber, iron, potassium and contains many vitamins.

Fresh Fruit Crumble

Topping:

I C flour
$\frac{3}{4}$ C brown or granulated sugar

$\frac{1}{2}$ C butter or margarine

Combine flour and sugar. Using a fork or your fingers, add butter or margarine. Blend well until mixed and crumbly.

Fillings Variations:

Italian Prune Plum

4 C Italian prune plums,
  pitted (12 to 14 plums)
$\frac{1}{4}$ C granulated sugar

I T flour
I tsp cinnamon
Rind of I orange, grated

Blueberry

4 C blueberries
I T lemon juice

I tsp cinnamon

Apple, Peach or Pear

4 C (6 medium) apples, peaches or
  pears, peeled, cored and sliced
I T lemon juice

I tsp cinnamon
$\frac{1}{2}$ C raisins (optional)

Combine desired filling ingredients in a greased I$\frac{1}{2}$-quart casserole or pie plate. Sprinkle with topping. Bake at 350° for 35 to 45 minutes, or until fruit is tender and topping is golden. Serve warm, with ice cream, frozen yogurt or whipped cream.

■ ■

Mom's Rugelach

Dough:

1 pkg dry yeast
1 T sugar
$\frac{1}{2}$ C warm milk (105° to 115°)

3 C flour
$\frac{1}{2}$ lb butter or margarine
3 egg yolks

Nut Mixture:

1 C walnuts, finely chopped
1 C sugar

2 tsp cinnamon

Filling:

12 to 14 oz jam

1 C raisins or mini-chocolate chips

Topping:

1 egg white beaten with $\frac{1}{2}$ tsp water

Dissolve yeast and sugar in warm milk. Cover and set aside until yeast mixture is bubbly. Place flour in a large mixing bowl. Using a fork or pastry blender, cut butter or margarine into it. Add yeast mixture and egg yolks and mix until smooth. Divide dough into 6 parts. Sprinkle the nut mixture on the board or counter on which you are going to roll out the dough. Roll out 1 piece of dough at a time into a rectangle. Place jam and raisins over dough and roll up jellyroll fashion. Brush with egg white mixture. Sprinkle with more nut mixture. Place on greased cookie sheets and slice into $\frac{3}{4}$-inch pieces. Spread out so that pieces are not touching each other. Cover with a towel and let rise for 20 to 30 minutes. Bake at 375° for 20 to 25 minutes, or until golden. Remove from cookie sheet and cool on a wire rack.

Hint: You can use any flavor jam and either dark or golden raisins. My favorite combinations are apricot jam with raisins and seedless raspberry jam with mini-chocolate chips. After the rugelach are cooled, transfer them to a tin where they will keep for a week at room temperature or for a few months in the freezer.

Orange Cookies

1 C butter or margarine	$1\frac{1}{2}$ C flour
1 C sugar	1 tsp baking powder
1 egg	Dash salt
1 tsp orange extract	2 tsp orange rind, grated

Cream butter or margarine and sugar until fluffy. Add egg and orange extract. In a separate bowl, sift flour, baking powder and salt together. Fold into creamed mixture. Add orange rind. Drop only 9 teaspoonfuls of dough onto each cookie sheet because the batter spreads. Bake at 350° for 10 to 12 minutes, or until edges are golden. Cool on a wire rack.

Yield: $4\frac{1}{2}$ dozen cookies

Hint: *These are also delicious made with lemon extract and lemon rind.*

Shortcut Cannoli

Dip:

1 lb ricotta cheese	Chopped pistachio nuts, chocolate
$\frac{3}{4}$ C confectioners' sugar	sprinkles or grated orange
2 tsp vanilla	peel, for garnish

Combine ricotta, confectioners' sugar and vanilla and beat until smooth, about 5 minutes. Refrigerate. When serving, sprinkle with one of the garnishes.

Cannoli Triangles:

Canola oil	Confectioners' sugar, for
$\frac{1}{2}$ pkg (approx. 25) wonton wrappers	sprinkling on top

Cut wonton wrappers in half on the diagonal so that you get 2 triangles from each wonton wrapper. In a wok or deep saucepan, fry triangles in 2 inches of oil, turning over very quickly so that triangles get only slightly golden in color. Drain on paper towels and cool. To serve, sprinkle triangles with confectioners' sugar and use for dipping. Store triangles in a tightly covered tin.

Yield: 50 cannoli triangles

Hint: *If you want to make the edges of the wonton wrapper more decorative you can use a ravioli wheel instead of a knife to cut them in half. You can make both the cannoli triangles and filling a day or two before serving. For a whole package of wonton wrappers (approx. 50) you will need to double the filling recipe. The filling can also be used to fill traditional cannoli shells.*

■ ■

Cranapple Crustless Pie

$1\frac{1}{2}$ C cranberries
$1\frac{1}{4}$ C sugar, divided
Pinch cinnamon
$2\frac{1}{2}$ C apples, peeled and sliced
$\frac{1}{2}$ C raisins

$\frac{1}{2}$ C walnuts, chopped
$\frac{1}{2}$ C butter or margarine, melted
2 eggs
1 C flour

Topping:

1 T sugar mixed with 1 tsp cinnamon

Combine cranberries, $\frac{1}{2}$ cup of the sugar, cinnamon, apples, raisins and nuts. Pour into a greased and floured 9-inch pie plate. Whisk together melted butter or margarine, eggs and remaining sugar. Add flour and blend well. Pour over fruit mixture. Sprinkle with sugar and cinnamon topping. Bake at 350° for 45 to 50 minutes, or until apples are tender and pie is golden. Cool for 10 minutes and run a knife around edge of pan. When completely cool, cut into wedges. To serve warm, spoon out of the pan. Serve with vanilla ice cream, frozen yogurt or whipped cream.

Hint: *If you aren't great at making pie crusts, this is perfect for you!*

Pat-a-Pie Crust

$1\frac{1}{2}$ C flour
Dash salt
1 T sugar

$\frac{1}{2}$ C butter or margarine
1 egg
2 T ice water

In a medium bowl, combine flour, salt and sugar. Cut butter or margarine into chunks and add to bowl. Using a fork or pastry blender, blend in butter or margarine and add egg and water. Continue blending with a fork or your fingers just until the dough forms a ball. If time permits, chill dough for at least 30 minutes. Pull off pieces of the dough and pat into a 9-inch pie plate until the entire surface of the pie plate is covered. Refrigerate for 30 minutes. Pour filling into pie crust and bake as desired. If you want to completely prebake the shell, line the well-chilled pie crust with a sheet of foil. Fill with raw rice or beans. Place the pie plate on a cookie sheet and bake at 425° for 10 minutes. Remove the foil, rice or beans and reduce oven temperature to 375°. Bake crust for 10 to 15 additional minutes, or until golden. Cool and fill with desired filling.

Hint: *If you prefer not to pat the crust, roll dough out with a rolling pin and lay it into the pie plate. Trim edges, as needed.*

Strawberry Chiffon Pie

Crust:

Approximately one-quarter of a sponge cake, cut into $\frac{1}{2}$" to $\frac{3}{4}$" slices

Line bottom and sides of a 10-inch pie plate or springform pan with cake. Decorate with fresh strawberries, if desired.

Filling:

10 oz pkg frozen strawberries, defrosted
$\frac{3}{4}$ C sugar ($\frac{1}{2}$ C if using strawberries in syrup)
2 egg whites, unbeaten
$\frac{1}{8}$ tsp salt

1 T lemon juice
$\frac{1}{3}$ C medium or all-purpose cream, whipped
1 tsp vanilla
Strawberries, for garnish (optional)

In a large mixing bowl, combine berries, sugar, egg whites, salt and lemon juice. Beat at medium speed for 15 minutes, or until stiff. In another bowl, whip cream and vanilla until stiff and fold into berry mixture. Pour onto sponge cake-lined pan. Garnish with strawberries, if desired. Freeze for several hours. Remove from freezer 45 minutes to 1 hour before serving.

Hint: **Orange Sponge Cake** *(pg. 158) or lady fingers can be used to line the pan throughout the year. Use Passover sponge cake during Passover. You can also vary this by using different berries.*

Yummy Fruit Dip

8 oz frozen whipped topping, thawed
8 oz strawberry yogurt
2 T sour cream

3 oz pkg strawberry Jello
$\frac{1}{2}$ to 1 tsp cinnamon, or to taste

Place all ingredients in a large bowl and whisk together until well blended. If possible, chill for a few hours before serving. Serve with fresh strawberries, melon, pineapple, etc.

Hint: *You can change the flavor and color of the dip by varying the yogurt and Jello flavors. To reduce the fat and calories, use light whipped topping, reduced fat sour cream, nonfat yogurt and sugar free Jello.*

■ ■ ■ ● ■ ■ ■ ■ □ ■ ● ■ ■ ■ ■ ■ ■ ■ ■ ■ ■ □ ■ ● ■ ■ □ ■ ■ ■

Apple Crumb Pie

Crust and Topping:

$1\frac{1}{2}$ C flour
$\frac{1}{2}$ C sugar

$\frac{1}{2}$ C butter or margarine
Pinch salt

Filling:

3 lbs apples (Cortland, Macoun or
  Baldwin) peeled, cored and sliced
1 T lemon juice, or to taste

$\frac{1}{2}$ C sugar
2 T cornstarch
1 tsp cinnamon

In a large bowl, combine flour, sugar, butter or margarine and salt. Using your hands, rub ingredients until it resembles fine crumbs. Remove 1 cup of the crumbs and set aside. Pat remaining crumbs in the bottom and up the sides of a 9-inch pie plate. Place sliced apples in a large bowl and drizzle with lemon juice. Shake apples so that they are all coated with juice. Combine sugar, cornstarch and cinnamon. Pour over apples. Mix well. Place in the crumb-lined pie plate. Bake at 425° for 20 minutes. Reduce oven temperature to 350° and pour reserved cup of crumb mixture over pie. Bake an additional 30 minutes, or until pie is golden brown. If desired, serve with vanilla ice cream, frozen yogurt or whipped cream.

Hint: *This pie is perfect for the person who doesn't like to make pie crusts. It is easy and delicious.*

Microwave Double Applesauce

5 apples, peeled, cored and quartered
2 to 3 T sugar, or to taste

$\frac{1}{2}$ C apple cider
$\frac{1}{2}$ tsp cinnamon

Place all ingredients in a large microwave bowl and mix. Cover with plastic wrap in which you have poked a hole. Microwave on high for 8 to 10 minutes, or until apples are tender. Blend with a fork until sauce is the consistency you desire. Sauce will thicken as it cools.

Hint: *This tastes like apple pie without the crust!*

Mud Pie

Crust:

$1\frac{1}{2}$ C chocolate cookies or wafers   6 T butter or margarine, melted

Crush cookies in a food processor or blender and add melted butter or margarine. Blend well. Pat into a 9-inch pie plate. Freeze for at least 2 hours.

Filling:

1 to $1\frac{1}{2}$ qts coffee ice cream, softened

Pour softened ice cream into the frozen chocolate crust. Freeze until firm

Fudge Sauce:

14 oz can sweetened condensed milk   2 squares unsweetened chocolate

Combine condensed milk and chocolate in a double boiler and stir until melted. Allow fudge sauce to cool to room temperature, or even refrigerate briefly, before spreading the sauce over the frozen ice cream. Return pie to the freezer. If you like, after the pie is completely frozen, decorate it with whipped cream, or garnish it with whipped cream when serving. One hour before serving, transfer the pie from the freezer to the refrigerator.

Hint: To microwave **Fudge Sauce**, combine condensed milk and chocolate and cook on high for $2\frac{1}{2}$ to 3 minutes, stirring occasionally. If you prefer, you can use **Ice Cream Parlor Fudge Sauce** (pg. 191) or **Chocolate Marshmallow Sauce** (pg. 190). Make sure the sauce is cool before spreading it on the pie.

Frozen Yogurt Pie

Crust:

1½ C (4 to 5 oz) chocolate cookies   2½ to 3 T butter or margarine, melted

Crush cookies into crumbs in a food processor or blender. Set aside 2 tablespoons of the crumbs. Mix remaining crumbs with melted butter or margarine and press into a 9-inch pie plate. Bake at 350° for 8 to 10 minutes, or until set. Remove from the oven and cool on a wire rack.

Filling:

8 to 10 oz fudge sauce,   1½ qts frozen yogurt
  at room temperature

Soften half the frozen yogurt and spread over cookie crust. Chill until firm. Spread fudge sauce over frozen yogurt. Freeze until set. Spread remaining half of softened frozen yogurt over fudge sauce. Chill until firm. Sprinkle with reserved 2 tablespoons cookie crumbs. Transfer from freezer to refrigerator about 1 hour before serving.

Hint: *You can make this low in fat if you use fat free or reduced fat cookies, fat free fudge sauce and fat free frozen yogurt. Use 15 or 16 low fat chocolate sandwich cookies or 1½ cups reduced fat chocolate graham crackers for a low fat crust. Use 2 flavors of frozen yogurt to add interest.*

Fresh Fruit Frozen Yogurt

2 C peaches or berries, puréed   1 tsp vanilla
1 egg white   1 C yogurt (not frozen)
⅓ to ½ C sugar

Combine puréed fruit, egg white, sugar and vanilla in a large mixing bowl. Beat at high speed for 5 to 7 minutes, or until almost doubled in volume. Fold in yogurt. Pour into a freezer container and cover. Freeze for 3 to 4 hours, or until firm. If desired, let soften for about 10 minutes before serving.

Hint: *The easiest way to purée the fruit is in a food processor or blender.*

Tropical-Style Mangoes

2 large mangoes, peeled
    and sliced or cubed
2 T brown sugar

2 T rum
2 T coconut, toasted (optional)
Vanilla or peach frozen yogurt or ice cream

Place mangoes in a bowl. Sprinkle with brown sugar and rum. Cover and refrigerate for 30 minutes to 1 hour. To serve, place mango slices or cubes in shallow dessert dishes and sprinkle with coconut, if desired. Top with a scoop of frozen yogurt or ice cream.

Hint: *Mangoes are low in calories and high in vitamins A and C. They are one of the most popular fruits in the world. For this recipe fresh mangoes are preferred, however you can use frozen mango cubes which have been defrosted. To keep this dessert fat free, omit the coconut and use fat free frozen yogurt.*

Three Berry Medley

1 C raspberries
1 C strawberries
1 C blueberries or blackberries

1 T honey
$\frac{1}{4}$ C orange juice
Coarsely chopped mint, to taste (optional)

Wash, drain and remove stems from berries. Whisk honey and juice together and pour over berries. If possible, marinate in refrigerator for a few hours. Remove from refrigerator 20 to 30 minutes prior to serving. If desired, sprinkle with mint. Serve this alone or over ice cream, frozen yogurt, angel cake, pound cake or **Chocolate Cheese Cake** (pg. 161).

Hint: *Frozen berries, which have been defrosted, may be substituted for fresh ones.*

Melon Vice Versa

1 cantaloupe
1 honeydew

Fresh strawberries and/or mint sprigs

Cut melons in half lengthwise and remove seeds. Cut each half into 4 wedges (2, if small). With melon baller, remove 3 or 4 balls from each wedge in a straight line. Fit cantaloupe balls into honeydew and vice versa! When serving, place melon wedges on a platter alternately in a circle. Garnish with strawberries and/or mint sprigs.

Hint: *Ordinary melon looks spectacular served this way! This can be used as an appetizer or dessert.*

■ ■

Apple Raisin Bread Pudding

2 T butter
2 C (about 2 medium) apples,
  cored and chopped
3 C (about 3 slices) day-old
  bread cubes
$\frac{1}{2}$ C raisins

4 eggs
2 C milk
$\frac{1}{3}$ C brown sugar, firmly packed
1 tsp vanilla
$\frac{1}{2}$ tsp nutmeg
Whipped cream or ice cream (optional)

Melt butter in a small saucepan over medium heat. Stir in apples. Cover and cook over medium heat, stirring occasionally, until slightly soft, about 5 to 7 minutes. In a greased, shallow $1\frac{1}{2}$-quart casserole, lightly toss together apples, bread cubes and raisins. In a medium bowl, beat together eggs, milk, brown sugar, vanilla and nutmeg until the sugar is dissolved. Pour over the bread mixture. Cover and refrigerate for several hours, or overnight. Bake, uncovered, in a preheated 350° oven for 45 to 55 minutes, or until a toothpick, inserted in the center, comes out clean. Serve hot, warm or chilled. Garnish with whipped cream, if desired.

Hint: *For the best flavor and texture, use challah (egg bread) or Italian bread. If you cut this recipe in half, bake for about 45 minutes.*

Bananas Foster

2 large ripe bananas
2 tsp lemon juice
3 T butter
$\frac{1}{3}$ C brown sugar

$\frac{1}{2}$ tsp cinnamon
2 T banana liqueur
2 T rum
4 scoops vanilla ice cream or frozen yogurt

Peel bananas and halve lengthwise. Drizzle lemon juice over them. In a large skillet, melt butter and brown sugar. Sprinkle with cinnamon. Add bananas and cook until barely tender, constantly spooning juice over, about 4 to 5 minutes. In another small pan, heat liqueur and rum. While tilting the pan, light a match to it. While the liquid is flaming, pour it over the bananas. When flame has died out, transfer bananas to 4 serving plates and top each with ice cream or frozen yogurt.

Hint: *A flaming dessert is very dramatic looking, however it is best to use long matches and be "very careful" when pouring the flaming liqueur.*

Strawberry Angel Dessert

11 oz angel food cake
1 pt fresh strawberries, sliced
3 oz pkg strawberry Jello

8 oz frozen whipped topping, defrosted or
1 C all-purpose cream, beaten until stiff
Few whole strawberries, for garnish

With your hands, break angel cake into random-size pieces. Place in a large glass bowl. Add strawberries and mix. Make Jello according to the directions on the package. Ladle about half of the liquid Jello over the cake and berries, pressing down to make sure the cake is covered. Refrigerate. Allow the remainder of the Jello to cool and begin to thicken. Whisk this Jello into the whipped topping or whipped cream until it is well blended. Spread it over the top of the cake until the cake is completely covered and the mixture is used up. Garnish with a few strawberries. Return to the refrigerator and allow to set for several hours before serving.

Hint: This dessert is very light and refreshing. To reduce the calories and fat, use low fat whipped topping. If you buy the angel cake, instead of making it, and use whipped topping, this dessert takes no time to make!

Top-of-the-Stove Fruit Shortcake

1 egg
2 T sugar
$\frac{1}{2}$ C milk
2 C all-purpose baking
    mix (i.e. Bisquick)

Few T flour
$\frac{1}{2}$ C apricot or peach jam or orange
    marmalade or combination
2 tsp confectioners' sugar

Beat egg and fold in remaining ingredients just until blended. Grease or spray a heavy 10-inch fry pan and preheat on stove over low heat. Knead dough and pat or roll out dough on a floured surface to a circle that will fit into the fry pan. Using a floured finger tip, make circle-like depressions in dough and fill with jam. Transfer to the preheated fry pan and cook, covered, on the lowest heat setting, for about 17 to 20 minutes, or until bottom is golden and top is firm to the touch. Remove from heat and dust with confectioners' sugar. Cut into 6 to 8 wedges and serve with strawberries, blueberries or any sliced fresh fruit. Garnish with whipped cream or nondairy topping, if desired.

Hint: You won't have to heat up your oven to make this old-fashioned shortcake!

Berries With Balsamic Vinegar

1 pt strawberries, raspberries,
blackberries or combination

$2\frac{1}{2}$ T light brown or granulated sugar
1 T balsamic vinegar

Wash, remove stems and slice berries. Toss with sugar and vinegar. Chill for at least 1 hour before serving. This is delicious by itself or it may be served over vanilla ice cream or frozen yogurt.

Hint: *This is an elegant and refreshing dessert that is effortless to prepare.*

Variation:

Caramelized Nut Topping for Balsamic Berries

2 T granulated sugar

3 T pine nuts or slivered almonds

Combine sugar and nuts in a small fry pan. Stir over medium heat until sugar melts and nuts are golden and glazed, about 4 to 5 minutes. Transfer to a foil-lined plate or cookie sheet and cool. Scoop vanilla ice cream or frozen yogurt into fruit dishes or champagne glasses. Top with balsamic berries and caramelized nuts.

Warm Pineapple Dessert

$\frac{1}{4}$ lb butter or margarine
$\frac{3}{4}$ C sugar
8 to 10 slices white bread,
crusts removed and cubed

4 eggs
20 oz can crushed pineapple
in its own juice, <u>un</u>drained

Cream butter or margarine with sugar until fluffy. Add eggs and beat until well blended. Fold in bread, pineapple and juice. Pour into a greased 9"x13" pan and bake at 350° for 1 hour, or until top is golden. Serve warm. Garnish with whipped cream or vanilla ice cream, if desired.

Hint: *When someone described this recipe to me it didn't sound too appealing. She said that it is so delicious that she serves it at Thanksgiving and many of her family get-togethers. Well, I was finally convinced to try it and I'm very glad that I did.*

Frozen Eggnog Mousse

2 envelopes unflavored gelatin
I qt eggnog, divided
$\frac{1}{3}$ C bourbon or rum
2 tsp vanilla
2 C confectioners' sugar

I pt whipping cream
$\frac{3}{4}$ C toasted almonds, chopped
$\frac{1}{2}$ tsp nutmeg
Red or green maraschino
   cherries, for garnish

In a saucepan, sprinkle the gelatin over I cup of eggnog. Heat slowly, stirring until the gelatin is dissolved. Remove from heat. In a large bowl, combine gelatin mixture with the remaining eggnog, bourbon or rum and vanilla. Stir well. Chill until thickened, about 20 minutes. In a small bowl, beat sugar into the cream until soft peaks form. Fold whipped cream mixture into the gelatin mixture. Stir in nuts and nutmeg. Pour into a freezer-proof serving dish or individual sherbet glasses. Freeze for a minimum of 4 hours, or until firm. Garnish with cherries, if desired. About 30 minutes before serving, move the mousse from the freezer to the refrigerator.

Hint: *This is an elegant holiday dessert which can be made a week in advance! It is perfect for a large crowd because it can be frozen in individual portions or scooped out of a beautiful serving bowl.*

Chocolate Soufflé

3 T butter
2 to $2\frac{1}{2}$ T flour
I C milk, scalded and cooled
3 oz unsweetened chocolate, melted
3 T liqueur (coffee, orange, etc.)

4 egg yolks, well-beaten
$\frac{1}{2}$ C sugar
5 egg whites
Additional butter and sugar for soufflé dish
Confectioners' sugar, for sprinkling on top

Over low heat, melt the butter and whisk in the flour. Slowly add scalded milk. Cook, whisking continuously until a smooth, thick paste is formed. This may take up to 7 minutes. Remove from heat and let cool. Combine melted chocolate with sugar and mix well. Stir in liqueur and mix until smooth. Combine chocolate mixture with milk mixture. Add beaten yolks and mix well. Butter a 2-quart soufflé dish and sprinkle with sugar. (May be prepared in advance to this point.) Beat whites until very stiff. Fold one-third of the whites into chocolate mixture, then fold in remaining whites. Pour into a prepared soufflé dish. Bake at 375° for 25 to 35 minutes, depending on firmness desired. Sprinkle with confectioners' sugar. Serve with cold **Creme Anglaise** (pg. 189) or softly whipped cream.

Creme Anglaise

4 egg yolks (or I whole egg)
$\frac{1}{4}$ C sugar
Pinch salt

I C scalded milk
2 T liqueur, brandy or rum or
I tsp vanilla extract

In a heavy pan or double boiler, combine egg yolks or egg, sugar and salt. Whisk, just until combined. Over low heat, slowly stir in hot milk and cook, stirring constantly until foam and bubbles appear and mixture coats a spoon (165°). Remove from heat or it will curdle! Whisk constantly to stop the cooking. Add liqueur or extract. Serve warm over a soufflé, fruit or cake or chill and serve cold.

Hint: To save time and clean up, you can scald the milk in the microwave by cooking on high for $2\frac{1}{2}$ to 3 minutes.

Basic Cake Decorating Frosting

I heaping C white shortening
2 lbs confectioners' sugar
2 tsp vanilla extract

I tsp almond extract
Water
Few drops food coloring

In a large mixer, cream shortening and confectioners' sugar until fluffy. Add extracts. Add water, blending until desired consistency is reached. Add food coloring, if desired.

Hint: This amount of frosting will be enough to cover and decorate a 9-inch cake.

Drizzly Chocolate Frosting

I oz unsweetened chocolate
2 T butter

$\frac{3}{4}$ C confectioners' sugar
2 T warm milk

Melt chocolate and butter in a double boiler. Whisk in confectioners' sugar and milk until smooth. Immediately drizzle over a cooled 9- or 10-inch bundt, tube or round cake.

*Hint: This frosting sets very fast, so you must work quickly. This is delicious on **Poppy Seed Cake** (pg. 165), **Orange Sponge Cake** (pg. 158), **Kugelhopf** (pg. 155) or almost any plain cake.*

■■■■■■■■■■■■■■■■■■■■■■■■■■■■■■

Chocolate Candy Pizza

12 oz (2 C) chocolate chips
9 oz white chocolate, divided
2 C miniature marshmallows
1 C crispy rice cereal

1 C unsalted peanuts
$\frac{1}{3}$ C flaked coconut
1 tsp oil

Microwave chocolate chips and 6 ounces of the white chocolate in a large microwaveable bowl on high for 2 minutes. Stir and microwave for 1 to 2 more minutes, stirring every 30 seconds, until completely melted and smooth. Fold in marshmallows, cereal and peanuts. Pour onto a greased 12-inch pizza pan. Top with coconut. Microwave remaining 3 ounces white chocolate and oil on high for 30 to 40 seconds. Stir. Microwave for an additional 30 to 40 seconds, or until smooth. Drizzle over top of pizza. Refrigerate for at least 40 minutes, or until firm. To serve, slice into wedges.

Hint: *To make this more festive, especially at Christmas, sprinkle drained and halved red and green maraschino cherries over top before sprinkling with coconut and drizzling with white chocolate. Colored mini-marshmallows could be substituted for white ones. Other Christmas variations would be to use red and green M&Ms instead of cherries. For Hanukkah, you can use yellow and blue M&Ms.*

Chocolate Marshmallow Sauce

$\frac{1}{3}$ C milk
$\frac{1}{4}$ C butter or margarine
Dash salt

1 C chocolate chips
1 tsp vanilla
$7\frac{1}{2}$ oz marshmallow fluff

Combine milk, butter or margarine and salt in a saucepan and bring just to a boil, stirring constantly. Add chocolate chips and vanilla, stirring constantly, until smooth. Whisk in marshmallow fluff until well blended.

Hint: *This is delicious on ice cream, ice cream pie or ice cream balls rolled in coconut and frozen until serving time. The sauce keeps well in the refrigerator and should be reheated at serving time.*

Ice Cream Parlor Hot Fudge Sauce

$\frac{1}{2}$ C butter or margarine
3 oz unsweetened chocolate
$1\frac{1}{2}$ C sugar
$\frac{1}{2}$ C unsweetened cocoa

Dash salt
1 C all-purpose cream or evaporated milk
2 tsp vanilla

Melt butter or margarine and chocolate in a double boiler. Combine sugar, cocoa and salt. Add to pan of melted butter-chocolate mixture, stirring until smooth. Slowly add cream or evaporated milk and bring to a boil, stirring constantly. Immediately remove from heat and add vanilla.

Hint: *This sauce, which is thick and not overly sweet, is supposed to be the "secret recipe" of one of the oldest ice cream companies in Boston!*

Chocolate Fondue

9 oz milk chocolate (preferably "Toblerone" Swiss chocolate which contains tiny bits of nougat and crushed almonds)

1 oz unsweetened baking chocolate
$\frac{2}{3}$ C light cream
$\frac{1}{4}$ C cognac or other liqueur (optional)

Chop all chocolate into small pieces and put into a fondue pot or over a double boiler. Melt over low heat and add the cream, blending well. Add liqueur, if desired, and stir. Serve from the fondue pot or transfer mixture from double boiler to a fondue pot or a bowl placed on a hot plate or warming tray.

Have a selection of any of the following bite-size items for dipping into the chocolate:

banana slices
apple wedges
peach slices
strawberries
large seedless grapes
candied ginger

lady fingers
pieces of pound cake or sponge cake
marshmallows
dried apricots
macaroons, cut into bite-size pieces

Use long wooden picks or fondue forks to dip any of these items into the fondue.

■ ■

Index

A

■ ■

G

H

I

J

K

L

M

N

O

P

■ ■

4 Easy Ways to Order Additional Copies of
So Easy, So Delicious or From Ellie's Kitchen To Yours

Mail:
Denell Press
P.O. Box 1164
Framingham, MA 01701

Phone:
(508) 620-1009

Fax:
(508) 620-1009

E-mail:
denellpress@geocities.com *AOL*

		Quantity	Amount
So Easy, So Delicious	$16.95 each ×		$
From Ellie's Kitchen To Yours	$14.95 each ×		$
5% sales tax if delivered in MA			$
Gift wrap with enclosure card	$2.00 each ×		$
Shipping for first book		1 @	$ 3.00
Shipping for each additional book	$1.00 each ×		$
		Total	$

Method of payment:

☐ Check for $ _____ made payable to "Denell Press"

☐ VISA ☐ Mastercard

Credit card number: __ __ __ __ __ __ __ __ __ __ __ __ __ __ __ __

Credit card expires (mo./yr.): __ __ / __ __

Signature _____

Ordered by:

Name _____

Address _____

City _____ State _____ Zip _____

Evening Phone (in case we have questions) _____

Ship to: (if different than "ordered by")

Name _____

Address _____

City _____ State _____ Zip _____

Delivery: ☐ To arrive within approximately 2 weeks
☐ To arrive by _____

Other:

• For a personalized autographed copy,
  include the first name of recipient _____

• Inquire about quantity discounts for 5 or more books